THE
GREEN HORNET
STREETCAR DISASTER

The Green Hornet
Streetcar Disaster

CRAIG ALLEN CLEVE

NIU
PRESS
DeKalb, IL

© 2012 by Northern Illinois University Press

Published by the Northern Illinois University Press, DeKalb, Illinois 60115

Manufactured in the United States using acid-free paper.

All Rights Reserved

Design by Julia Fauci

Library of Congress Cataloging-in-Publication Data

Cleve, Craig Allen.

The Green Hornet streetcar disaster / Craig Allen Cleve.

p. cm.

Includes bibliographical references and index.

ISBN 978-0-87580-454-5 (cloth : acid-free paper) — ISBN 978-1-60909-058-6 (e-book)

1. Chicago (Ill.)—History—20th century. 2. Disasters—Illinois—Chicago—History—20th century. 3. Explosions—Illinois—Chicago—History—20th century. 4. Traffic accidents—Illinois—Chicago—History—20th century. 5. Traffic fatalities—Illinois—Chicago—History—20th century. 6. Electric railroad accidents—Illinois—Chicago—History—20th century. 7. Truck accidents—Illinois—Chicago—History—20th century. 8. Gasoline—Transportation—Illinois—Chicago—History—20th century. 9. Chicago (Ill.)—Biography. I. Title.

F548.5.C66 2012

977.3'11—dc23

2011052667

Contents

Preface

It has been more than 50 years since trolleys last clattered down Chicago streets carrying passengers to work or home or other destinations. Like phantoms, they appear in nostalgic stories told by parents and grandparents to children and grandchildren—stories of cherished trips to movie theaters, museums, and ballparks, all of which began and ended with a ride on a trolley.

This is a sad story, lost over time with the passing of the generations. Like an urban legend, it has been kept alive on barstools and told around kitchen tables, its facts often embellished at the discretion of the teller.

My mother was the first person to tell it to me.

One Sunday afternoon when I was still in elementary school, she happened to flip through the magazine section of the Sunday papers when a particular photograph caught her eye. "Take a look at this," she said to me, knowing my fascination with history even then. She handed me the magazine, folded in half, with the picture in question next to her thumb.

It was a black-and-white photo of something that looked like an old bus. It was cast sideways, blocking traffic on the street, and it looked like it had been through a war. All of its windows were broken, and the doors had been ripped apart. Debris littered the ground. Fire trucks and firemen were everywhere. Something awful had occurred.

"It was a streetcar crash that happened in 1950 or '51," my mother began. "A streetcar crashed into a gas truck. There was an explosion. A lot of people died."

She went on to tell me how my grandfather used to take that streetcar route every day, and how on the day of the accident, he had been called back into the boss's office and ended up leaving work a few minutes later than usual. She intimated that had he left work at his regular time, he might have been on that trolley.

I grew up believing that fate had intervened. Like the person who lets the full elevator car pass by because his gut tells him to do so, I thought my grandfather had somehow cheated death that night.

As a research tool, family lore is not without its flaws. Yet, the story stayed with me all my life, and after my first book was published, I decided to chase an old, forgotten Chicago ghost. It wasn't hard to find.

Near the end of the evening rush hour on May 25, 1950, one of the Chicago Transit Authority's new streamlined trolleys, known as "Green Hornets," collided with a gas truck on State Street at 62nd Place. The motorman of the trolley apparently failed to heed the warnings of a flagger positioned in front of a switch that was about to detour him around an obstacle.

The trolley, loaded nearly to capacity, entered the switch at an excessive speed, then slammed into the gas truck, which had yet to make its first delivery of the day and was hauling 8,000 gallons of gasoline. The gas caught fire and poured onto State Street, completely surrounding the trolley in a matter of seconds.

Miraculously, more than half of the passengers were able to escape the inferno by climbing out a rear window. But 33 people died, most of them crammed in front of the trolley's rear doors, which failed to stay open in the panic.

It was Chicago's worst traffic accident, and the worst two-vehicle traffic accident in U.S. history. Yet ask a Chicagoan about the Green Hornet Streetcar Disaster, and you'll likely get a puzzled look in response.

It was a well-documented event in both the local and national press. A month-long Coroner's Inquest determined the causes of the accident, and recommendations were made to the CTA and the Chicago City Council.

But unlike other Chicago disasters, very little changed as a result. Safety adaptations were made to the trolleys within a year, but most recommendations and calls for reform fell on deaf ears.

At the time of the accident, streetcars in Chicago were on the way out, and they were gone entirely within the decade. Without trolleys to remind them of what happened, the accident gradually receded from the collective consciousness. Perhaps more than any other major calamity in Chicago history, the Green Hornet Streetcar Disaster has survived for 60 years on hearsay and legend.

In the fall of 2004, I began to compile information related to the accident through newspaper archives and documents provided by the

Chicago Transit Authority. Shortly after, I searched for and found individuals who were there that day or whose lives were forever changed—
eyewitnesses, journalists, family members, and even survivors.

Together, they told a remarkable story about an accident that—like so
many others before and since—never should have happened. It took a
phenomenal combination of natural events, human error, and mechanical failure to create the circumstances necessary for disaster. Every causal
factor aligned perfectly, and nearly everything that could have gone
wrong, did.

Hours in developing, it was over in less than five minutes for each of
the 33 casualties, most of whom died within inches of safety and before
any rescue squads could arrive to help them.

They were ordinary people—an accurate cross-section of working-
class Chicago in 1950: men and women, old and young, black and white.
They were teachers and clerks, domestic servants and housewives, blue
collar and white collar. Almost all of them were heading home after a
typical work day.

They ought to be remembered.

The elements of catastrophe are always with us. We revisit tragedy
not because of some maudlin impulse, but because we are appalled by
it and wish to learn from it. In a history filled with tragic loss, the Green
Hornet Streetcar Disaster is one of Chicago's harshest lessons.

I have been diligent in my research, and I believe the events happened, to the best of my knowledge and efforts, as I portray them. Any
errors or oversights are entirely my own.

AUTHOR'S NOTE—With rare exception, newspapers in 1950 referred
to street railway vehicles as "trolleys." Most Chicagoans who rode them
remember them as "streetcars." I have chosen to use both terms, and for
the purposes of this book the reader should consider them synonymous.

Acknowledgments

Sixty years have elapsed since the Green Hornet Streetcar Disaster, and with the passing of each year, the number of people directly associated with the event gets smaller. I was most fortunate to talk with many people who were there that day in one capacity or another. This book could not exist without their contributions.

I was able to contact just two survivors of the accident—Robert Nalls and Kyteria Drish (nee Cooper). Mr. Nalls and I corresponded in the months just prior to his death. I had the privilege of interviewing Mrs. Drish, who told a haunting tale of escape from the trolley. The section on the parasitic practices of ambulance chasers was included after hearing her story.

I am indebted to the families of Paul Manning, Charles Kleim, and William Liddell—particularly to Mike Medley, nephew of Paul and son of Nell and Ray Medley; Douglas Kleim, grandson of Charles; and Mrs. Elsie Liddell, William's widow.

Steve Lasker graciously provided many of the photos included here. I am particularly grateful for the candor and clarity with which he shared his experiences as an amateur photographer in 1950 Chicago.

Dr. Sherman Beverly shared his memories of being a CTA motorman during the 1950s. He painted a clear picture of a motorman's typical day—from car barn to the streets to the car barn again.

Bruce Moffat was my contact person within the Chicago Transit Authority. He located many of the additional photos used in the book. He also provided me with a copy of the R. F. Kelly report that precisely detailed witness testimony at the Coroner's Inquest. An author of numerous books about transportation in Chicago, Bruce contributed his technical expertise regarding switches, turnarounds, and other CTA protocols.

I am also indebted to the fine staff in the Research Library of the Chicago History Museum, one of my favorite locations in the city.

THE
GREEN HORNET
STREETCAR DISASTER

just a few miles away. Since these trucks were based outside city limits, they were exempt from the compartmented tank rule.

The threat of serious accidents was omnipresent, but the exemption remained in place even as accidents occurred:

In 1938, a double-bottom gas truck from Whiting, Indiana collided with a watermelon truck at Ashland Avenue near Fulton Street. The uncompartmented tank ruptured, and all 6,500 gallons of gas caught fire. Miraculously, no injuries were reported. Trolley service along Ashland was interrupted for hours as the flames melted the overhead trolley wires.[6]

In 1943, another gas truck crashed into a concrete abutment at the entrance to a viaduct at 4600 W. 16th Street. The driver had been trying to go around an accident inside the viaduct when the collision occurred. The tank he was hauling ruptured, and the 1,500 gallons of gasoline began to spill onto the pavement in and around the viaduct. When a motorist stuck inside the viaduct tried to start his car and leave the scene, a spark from his vehicle ignited the fuel. The viaduct erupted in flames. The driver of the gas truck died, trapped within his vehicle. Two others, including a police officer who came to the truck driver's aid, were killed. Seventeen people were injured.[7]

In 1946, Chief Fire Marshal Anthony Mullaney warned the Chicago City Council of the dangers posed by large tractor-trailer trucks hauling gasoline through crowded city streets. He cited some 55 accidents involving gas trucks over a 10-year period and called for their banishment. A subcommittee was formed to investigate the claim, but no recommendation in favor of further regulating gasoline haulage was ever handed down.

Uncompartmented gas trucks continued to haul gasoline in Chicago throughout the decade of the 1940s and into the next.[8]

Though still operating in considerable numbers, the Chicago trolley was fast becoming an endangered species in 1950. Chicago was the biggest it would ever be with 3.6 million inhabitants, and the postwar migration to the suburbs was only just beginning. In spite of the availability of the automobile, many city dwellers did not yet own one and relied on public transportation on a daily basis.

Prior to World War II, Chicago's fleet of 3,500 trolleys was the largest in the world.[9] Laid end-to-end, Chicago trolley track would have extended to New York City and beyond. But by the war's end, more than 70 percent of the vehicles had lived beyond their useful lives. Many were more than 30 years old and needed to be replaced.[10] In addition to the looming costs of vehicle modernization, the annual cost of maintaining and replacing trolley track was enormous. These two conditions sealed the fate of the trolley in Chicago.

Chicago Surface Lines (CSL), the company that operated the trolleys prior to the creation of the Chicago Transit Authority, had already devised a plan to decommission trolleys in favor of gas-powered motor buses and electric trolley buses.[11] Two major factors prevented the implementation of the plan. The first was money. The CSL was bankrupt, operating at a $190 million deficit by the mid-1940s. The company had no funds with which to purchase new rolling stock, and no credit on which to borrow.[12] The second factor was World War II, during which production of nonessential vehicles was halted.

After the war, the CSL was consolidated with another financially troubled institution, the Chicago Rapid Transit Company, which ran the elevated system. As a condition of the consolidation into the new Chicago Transit Authority, the courts forgave a majority of the debt accumulated by both companies. The fledgling CTA managed to secure $25 million in revenue bonds and equipment trust certificates, a large portion of which was immediately designated toward replacing some of the dilapidated streetcars.[13]

Between 1946 and 1949, more than 15 different trolley routes were converted to motor and/or trolley buses. "The Street Car is Dead," proclaimed one cryptic editorial in 1946.[14] Indeed, it appeared that the death knell had sounded for the trolley in Chicago.

There was one exception. It was called the "Green Hornet."

Green Hornets were a variation on a popular, versatile trolley design called a Presidents' Conference Committee car, or "PCC."[15] They were the brainchild of some of the most talented minds in the street railway industry. First developed in the 1930s, they were inspired by the Art Deco movement and appeared sleek and streamlined alongside their boxy forerunners.

The older trolleys seated around 35 to 40 passengers. People sat on caned seats surrounded by a mostly wooden interior beneath decades of varnish and paint. The cars creaked and groaned at every start, stop, and turn. Most had domed ceilings that made them all the more cacophonous. They were poorly insulated and ventilated, freezing in winter and sweltering in summer.

Many Chicagoans looked upon them with nostalgia, particularly the old red trolleys, most of which had been built in the 1920s and went by nicknames like "Turtlebacks," "Big Brills," "169's," and "Red Rockets."[16] A few even lasted into the 1950s.

By contrast, the PCCs suggested grace and speed. They accelerated quickly and stopped smoothly. They contained more creature comforts too, including leather upholstery, good lighting, and a heating system that drew wasted heat from the car's motor. They were well insulated, which contributed to their quiet ride and earned them the reputation as "noiseless" vehicles.[17]

Within a decade, PCCs quickly became one of the most popular street railway vehicles in the country. By 1946, they were being used in many U.S. cities, including Baltimore, Boston, Brooklyn, Dallas, Philadelphia, Pittsburgh, San Francisco, St. Louis, and Washington, D.C.[18] Their designers were constantly looking for ways of improving the vehicles, and they proved to be remarkably adaptable to the specific needs of the cities that purchased them.

Prior to the war, the first 83 PCCs were used exclusively along busy Madison Avenue and met with great success,[19] but the Depression, the war, and the CSL's swelling debt prevented the company from purchasing more of the vehicles. In 1946, armed with the $25 million loan,[20] the CSL made its final vehicle purchase just prior to consolidating with the Chicago Rapid Transit Company to form the CTA.[21] It purchased 600 PCCs, earmarking them for the most heavily trafficked streets in the city.[22] In great part, they wagered the potential success of the vehicles on their versatility.

Many trolleys in Chicago employed a two-man operation, with a motorman in front and a conductor in the rear. Mechanical engineers experimented with the design of the PCCs to try to find a way of making the two-man operation more efficient.

They started by elongating the car, adding a ten-foot enclosed platform in the rear of the vehicle. Since the two-man operation used a rear entrance, engineers decided to enlarge the rear doors to ensure a faster loading time. A triple set of doors opened, revealing two steps up to the platform, which contained six additional seats winding along the rear windows. Passengers exited through doors located at the center and front of the car.

The doors themselves were of a uniquely innovative design. Each doorway consisted of two slender metal panels with a vertical row of small windows, and they were lined with a hard rubber gasket. They were fastened top and bottom along a central axis. A clever mechanism caused them to open without a push from boarding passengers. Rather, they swiveled open in one rapid movement. They were dubbed "blinker" doors because when viewed from the street, they resembled a blinking eye.

The blinker doors operated electronically, but the power source was not connected to the trolley's main power. If the wheel at the end of the long trolley pole became disconnected from the electric wire suspended above the street, the doors could still open. The device that opened the blinker doors was hooked to a self-contained battery.[23]

The rear platform flushed out the length of the Green Hornets to an even 50 feet. Seating capacity depended on the manufacturer and design and varied between 54 and 57 passengers with additional room for standees in the aisles and in the rear.[24] A full car might contain as many as 75 passengers—sometimes more during a particularly heavy rush hour.

Great care had been taken to ensure the safety of passengers as well as the safe operation of the vehicles. In this regard, PCCs were a vast improvement over their predecessors. But viewed through a twenty-first-century lens, they still had their flaws.

Unlike modern buses or trolleys, there were no designated emergency windows aboard the PCCs. No side windows opened outward. There were no ceiling hatches for a roof exit. There was no emergency rear door, nor was there an exit on the left-hand side of the vehicle. All PCCs had two large rear windows measuring about 26 by 27 inches.[25] A metal bar ran horizontally across each of them, dividing the opening in half. Both windows were hinged on the side and could open outward to provide an alternate exit. But a CTA policy kept at least one of the windows bolted shut at all times, presumably to dissuade horseplay or prevent damage to the windows themselves.[26]

Passenger windows coursed the sides of the vehicles. They opened via hand cranks located above the pane. Vigorous cranking raised the windows, which recessed into the roof. But covering the bottom half of each window was a steel "safety bar" fitted securely to deter passengers from sticking their hands and arms outside of the car. In Chicago, streetcars passed dangerously close to other vehicles, including other streetcars passing in the opposite direction. The threat to passengers' limbs was quite real.[27]

Between the safety bars and ceiling, a narrow gap of no more than six inches represented the only other potential exit from the vehicle and eliminated the possibility of anyone other than a small child from using them as a means of escape.

The Green Hornets debuted in 1947. The full complement of 600 vehicles was added over the next three years, as fast as the manufacturers could turn them out. Riders were given the opportunity to select the color scheme of the new models. Several of the older models were painted with different color combinations to help people decide. The winning combination proved to be a light Mercury Green on the bottom half and Croydon Cream for the top half, with a thin dividing line of Swamp Holly Orange.[28] The Green Hornet nickname followed soon after.

Traffic laws in Chicago had not yet evolved with the modern trolleys. Where their predecessors rumbled along at a pastoral pace, the new Green Hornets could easily match the posted speed limits on busy streets—usually between 25 and 30 mph. Some argued that the new cars could go even faster.

Trolleys were not subject to the same rules of the road as other motor vehicles. A Chicago traffic cop did not have the authority to stop a speeding trolley, principally because when such laws had been enacted decades before, the term "speeding trolley" was an oxymoron.[29]

Compounding the problem was the fact that streetcars did not contain speedometers. Although motormen were expected to conform to the rules of the road, the speed at which a new Green Hornet operated was based on the judgment—sound or faulty—of its operator. Naturally, some motormen took liberties.

Speed made the Hornets particularly dangerous in light of the limited maneuverability of the vehicles. Operating on rails, they could not voluntarily move to the left or right. Their braking system was the best available, but they could not stop as quickly as rubber tires on pavement. Motorists sometimes seemed to forget that the trolleys were even there, regularly darting in front of or around the vehicles without regard for the latter's ability to avoid them. As progressively more motor vehicles hit the streets, collisions between trolleys and other vehicles became more frequent. By 1950, just three years after their introduction to Chicago streets, it was unusual to find a Green Hornet that was not battle-scarred from a confrontation with another motor vehicle.

Prior to the accident on May 25, 1950, accidents involving Green Hornets and gas trucks had occurred. On February 6, 1948, a fuel truck struck a trolley at 59th Street and Damen Avenue. No injuries were reported, and although the truck's tank ruptured, the truck was carrying oil instead of gasoline.[30]

Five days later, on February 11, four people were injured in a trolley/fuel truck collision at 79th Street and Ashland Avenue. Once again, the truck involved was carrying oil.[31]

Less than three weeks later, on March 1, a Green Hornet struck a gas truck on Western Avenue. This time, the truck was hauling gasoline, which burst into flames. Luckily, the trolley was nearly empty, and the motorman, conductor, and seven passengers were able to exit through the rear doors.[32]

Then, on October 26, 1948, at the intersection of 63rd and State streets, a Green Hornet rear-ended a gas truck, causing gasoline to pour from the damaged vehicle. No one was injured. However, moments after the collision, the gasoline, which had drained into nearby sewers, found an ignition source—perhaps from a discarded cigarette—and exploded in a ball of fire. One pedestrian was injured when the blast knocked her from her feet.[33]

In spite of clear records detailing collisions between streetcars and gas trucks within a short period of time, no steps were taken to regulate the travel of either vehicle. To that point, all of the accidents had been relatively minor with regard to property damage and injury.

But all of that was about to change.

Chapter
TWO

If it had not rained on May 25, 1950, the Green Hornet Streetcar Disaster never would have happened. Chicago's worst traffic accident was as much about a flooded viaduct as it was about two vehicles involved in a deadly collision. It was spring in Chicago, and the city was in the throes of a heat wave. Tuesday, Wednesday, and Thursday of that week had all seen temperatures in excess of 80 degrees. On Thursday morning, the day of the accident, the temperature had topped out at 92 degrees.

Shortly after 2:00 p.m., a particularly ferocious storm cell swept through the city, dumping a large amount of water on its streets in a short amount of time.[1] The city's antiquated sewer system could not handle such a quick inundation, and in several places, streets, tunnels, and viaducts flooded.[2]

One viaduct notorious for flooding was located just south of the intersection of State and 63rd streets, beneath the tracks of the Pennsylvania Railroad. At that point, State Street made a gradual downward slope as it passed beneath the tracks. After severe storms, it sometimes flooded with as much as three feet of water.[3]

The viaduct was a particular nuisance to Southsiders who relied on trolley service along State Street. When it came to rain, trolleys were deceptive vehicles. Boasting enough speed and weight to ford through a flooded viaduct, they were hobbled by their electric motors, which were located beneath their floors. Standing water of only a few inches made detours necessary. High-water marks were painted on the sides of viaducts to help motormen determine whether or not passage was safe.

As a fail-safe, the CTA maintained turnaround loops along many of its routes. Turnaround loops were like a streetcar version of an expressway cloverleaf. By means of a switch, a detoured car entered the turnaround—usually a loop of track that ran along the perimeter of a vacant lot or alley network—and exited traveling in the opposite direction. In the case of the viaduct at 63rd Street, the turnaround loop served the dual purpose of detouring trolleys when the viaduct flooded, as well as "short-turning" trolleys when passenger usage south of 63rd Street was particularly light.[4]

Detoured cars normally continued to their intended destinations, but by different routes. "Short-turning" was more common. A short-turned car used the turnaround to change direction and head back to its point of origin. Until the obstacle was removed, the turnaround became the temporary end-of-the-line.

Around 2:30 p.m., Peter Duggan, the CTA supervisor on duty at the turnaround, noticed that the viaduct there was flooded and impassable.[5] He phoned headquarters and described the scene. It was decided that all southbound trolleys on State would be short-turned, using the turnaround at 62nd Place.

Duggan asked for assistance, knowing that the task before him was tedious. He would have to flag down every southbound trolley and alert them of the short-turn. Once the vehicles had stopped, he would bark instructions to their motormen, and then open the switch to the turnaround. Switch boxes were located beneath access panels in the street. A metal handle was inserted, and when a supervisor pulled on it, the switch opened and the car entered the turnaround.

That accomplished, the supervisor closed the switch and watched for the next trolley, repeating the process as needed.

As trolley traffic increased, many supervisors resorted to plugging the switch.

"Plugging" referred to the practice of inserting a wood block or bolt beneath an upraised switch handle, thus allowing the switch to remain in the open position. It saved time, and it spared the supervisor the physical exertion of opening and closing the switch with each arrival.

But plugging was frowned upon by the CTA.[6] When a switch was plugged, the supervisor or flagger positioned there could not abandon his post. The three-foot iron handle rose from the pavement at about a 30-degree angle. Without someone in position, a passing automobile might clip the handle, causing damage to both the vehicle and the switch. Moreover, if a motorman somehow missed a flagger's signals, the vehicle could enter an open switch at an excessive speed, perhaps causing it to derail.

Over time, turnarounds became favorite places for motormen to make up for lost time. Most supervisors patrolled turnarounds in cars. Few, if any, turnarounds had supervisors stationed there round the clock. CTA rules stipulated that a motorman should approach a turnaround at a safe speed. It was generally agreed that a motorman could tell if a switch was open within a car length of the switch—a distance of roughly 50 feet. A safe speed within which a motorman could make that determination and slow or stop was estimated at 5 mph.[7]

Some motormen disregarded this rule. Unless a flagger or supervisor was visible, many continued at their normal speed. In spite of the rule, the switch at State Street and 62nd Place remained plugged all afternoon, and Duggan hoped his flagger would arrive shortly.

CTA employee Charles Kleim was dispatched to the turnaround loop at 62nd Place, and he arrived there at 2:45 p.m. Kleim was 45, and he had worked at the CTA for nine years. He was a meticulous, hardworking ex-marine sergeant, who worked as a pharmacist's assistant at a local drug store when he wasn't driving a bus. He favored dress shirts and ties even on his off days, and he worked hard to provide for his wife and two children.[8]

Most days, Kleim drove a bus. His day had begun at 3:30 a.m. when he left the South Side car barn at 77th Street and Vincennes Avenue and began his regular route. He returned to the barn after working an eight-hour shift.

His supervisor asked him to remain at the barn in case he had extra work for him.[9] It was not an unusual request. Bad weather had been forecast, and Kleim thought he might be asked to work an extra shift. His wife was having medical problems, and he could certainly use the extra money.[10]

Once at the turnaround, Duggan explained the situation and asked Kleim to flag down all southbound trolleys. The supervisor positioned himself inside the turnaround. With two men working the scene, multiple cars could enter the turnaround at the same time, preventing a logjam of vehicles at the entrance.

Kleim didn't have any flags, but that was not unusual. He had no flares or smudge pots. He wore his typical CTA garb: navy blue slacks, light blue shirt, navy tie, and a navy blue motorman's cap with a CTA badge. The temperature had dropped more than 20 degrees after the rain, and Kleim may have worn a light, tan jacket he had brought with him that morning.[11]

Before he took his post, he noticed that the switch was plugged. If he thought anything of it, he did not say so. Kleim was a veteran, and he knew the drill.

It was slow but efficient work, and Kleim hoped it would end soon. He was disappointed. After just an hour or so at the switch, the skies opened again with a second downpour. As with the first storm, the rain didn't last long. But enough rain fell to prompt the Department of Streets and Sanitation to dispatch a crew to the viaduct. They began the slow task of draining the underpass, using an electric-powered pump. It would take at least another two hours to clear the viaduct and resume streetcar travel.[12]

By the time the evening rush hour neared its end, Kleim had safely flagged down more than 200 trolleys in about four hours.[13] He had been on the job for more than 15 hours, and his work was almost finished. By 6:30 p.m., trucks and cars had resumed passage through the viaduct. Word came from the crew that the waters had reached a nearly passable depth for trolleys.[14] Within another 15 or 20 minutes, trolley service would be able to continue. For Charles Kleim, it was the best news he had heard all day. The worst news, however, was yet to come.

Rain was falling at 4 p.m. when Paul Manning left his North Side home bound for the trolley barn at Devon Avenue and Clark Street. Manning was a veteran CTA motorman who did not own an automobile. As an employee of the CTA, Manning rode public transportation for free. He had worked for the company since the end of the war, piloting street-cars as well as buses.[15]

As part of a familiar ritual, Manning was accompanied on the trip by his wife, Mamie. The couple had been married nearly 20 years— childhood sweethearts back in Mississippi who had married young and remained best friends. As they hurried through the downpour, there was nothing in Paul Manning's demeanor that suggested he was distant or distracted.

Manning was 42, tall, lanky, and handsome, with dark hair, a cleft chin, and a look of mischief in his eyes. Mamie Manning was two years younger, vivacious and pretty on her worst day. The Mannings had no children.

Paul Manning had served in the Navy during WWII, and four years later, he and his wife were enjoying the most stable, prosperous time of their lives. They shared a duplex on Berwyn Avenue with Mamie's younger sister, Nell, and her husband, Ray Medley, also a CTA motorman. The house on Berwyn was about two miles from the barn where both Manning and Medley worked.

Manning had an average CTA service record, which is to say he did his job well and had good attendance. Over an 18-month stretch leading up to the accident, he had been involved in ten accidents involving trolleys and buses that he had been operating. It was an excessive number on paper, but records indicate that only two of the ten accidents were chargeable to Manning, both of which had resulted in very minor damage and no injuries.[16]

He missed work due to the occasional cold, but he was otherwise in good health. He and his wife belonged to a strict Pentecostal church which, among other things, forbade the use of alcohol. Earlier in the month of May, he had taken a two-week leave of absence to visit his ailing mother in Mississippi. He returned to work on May 15.

The Mannings continued down Berwyn to the nearest bus stop at California Avenue. They boarded a northbound bus and rode it to Devon Avenue, where they transferred to an eastbound bus that carried them to the corner of Devon and Clark streets. Here, Manning kissed his wife good-bye and disembarked, walking north on Clark for half a block to the barn. His wife remained on board the bus as it crossed Clark and for another block east to Bosworth, where she got off to do some shopping.

On days when she accompanied her husband on his trip to work, the Mannings frequently engaged in a curious game of cat-and-mouse.[17] Mamie Manning did her shopping at the markets along Devon Avenue, knowing she had about 30 minutes before her husband was due to leave the barn and head east along the avenue on his first run of the day. As the appointed time approached, she would sometimes wait on the sidewalk outside the market watching for her husband's trolley.

Shortly after 5 p.m., Manning's car would exit the barn onto Clark Street and travel less than half a block to Devon. A left turn later and he began to search the sidewalks for his wife. She was never hard to find.

When he saw her, he would ring the trolley's bell in salutation, but also as an invitation. As he eased the car alongside the safety island at Bosworth where his first passengers of the day began to board, Mamie remained on the sidewalk and engaged in some quick mental gymnastics. If she had the time, she would board the car—groceries and all—and take a seat behind her husband, keeping him company on his first trip through the circuit.

If she had no time, or if she had perishables in her bag, she would dismiss him with a friendly wave and watch him as he continued down Devon toward Lake Michigan.

Manning's route, the No. 36-Broadway/State, very nearly ran the length of the city from top to bottom. It followed a somewhat meandering path for about 16.5 miles including a long stretch through downtown Chicago along State Street. The full circuit from north to south and back again took about four hours to complete, depending on time of day. Manning completed the circuit twice during a normal shift.[18]

The Clark/Devon car barn had been in operation since 1901. It was a two-story structure whose most prominent feature included four enormous doorways through which streetcars entered and exited via Clark Street. In addition to the Broadway-State route, the Western Avenue line and the Clark-Wentworth line also operated out of the barn in 1950.

Manning was glad to be a veteran motorman. Rookies worked swing shifts, often picking up their route assignments at the barn just moments before heading out on a run. A rookie might have to travel an unfamiliar route, not knowing when or where to expect the largest number of passengers. It was easy for a rookie to fall behind schedule.

"Make your time" was a sort of company motto. It was a reminder to all motormen to adhere as precisely as possible to one's schedule—neither ahead nor behind. And although the union contract stipulated otherwise, a motorman who did not consistently make his time was sometimes passed over when the plum assignments were passed out.[19]

Under no circumstances did the company ever emphasize schedules over safety. Safe operation of its vehicles was always viewed with paramount importance. However, the company's rigorous reminders of remaining on time may have caused some motormen to occasionally sacrifice safety as they tried to make up time.

Manning had been a motorman long enough to know the tricks of his trade. An experienced motorman, he had intimate knowledge of his route. There would be places on every trip where he would likely lose time taking on passengers, especially downtown during rush hour. But he also knew where the lulls were—stretches where few passengers boarded. Here, he could put on a little extra speed and make up lost time.[20] In this regard, his speedy new Green Hornet was a godsend.

Where Manning's job was clear—safe operation of the vehicle within designated time parameters—the yeoman's job was performed by the car's conductor. Shortly before leaving the barn, Manning was joined by William Liddell, a conductor with whom he had worked before. Liddell was 29 years old and lived with his wife in nearby Evanston. Liddell was African-American, and at the time his job as conductor was the best available within the company for a man of color. The CTA had not yet hired its first black motorman. Like Manning, Liddell was a transplant from Mississippi.

Unlike Manning, he had just three years with the company and was still working swing shifts. His week was a smorgasbord of different routes and haphazard schedules. He was happy to be working consistently out of the Clark/Devon barn, but he hoped for a regular route and schedule. It would be years before he and his wife could attend Sunday church or celebrate Christmas together.[21]

Liddell had already completed a circuit on the Clark/Wentworth route before joining Manning. He boarded car No. 7078 and made a quick pass through the aisle, checking for trash. He filled his coin belt with the requisite amount of change, which he provided himself. He checked his uniform and other equipment, including a chrome-plated hole punch and a pocket full of transfer slips.

Liddell's station was at a seat directly opposite the triple doors at the rear of the car. There was a conductor's seat, but a conductor seldom did much sitting as he took fares, issued transfers, gave directions, and made sure the doors were clear before they closed and the car continued. He assisted passengers with boarding, handled difficult passengers with tact, and kept the brunt of distraction away from the motorman at the front of the car.

Liddell was also in charge of opening and closing the rear doors of the vehicle.

In front of Liddell and just to his right was a small, round control panel with chrome handles. It was mounted on a pedestal, and it looked like an odd hybrid of parking meter and ship captain's wheel. Its face contained a row of six small levers, the first two of which opened the rear doors when pressed. An emergency lever inches to his right opened the doors in the event of a power failure.[22]

At 5:05 p.m., as Manning eased the Green Hornet out of the barn and onto Clark Street, neither he nor Liddell had any idea that the rain had caused a viaduct to flood at 63rd and State streets.[23]

After proceeding a short distance to the corner, Manning completed a left-hand turn onto Devon, where he immediately began to search for his wife. She was waiting on the sidewalk across from the safety island at Bosworth. Manning stopped the vehicle and the first few passengers boarded through the rear entrance. Liddell took their fares, dispensing transfers when requested and clicking out the proper change with his coin changer.

Manning clanged the trolley's bell and opened the front doors to get a better look at his wife. He smiled his mischievous smile at her. She returned the smile and waved at him. Manning must have interpreted the wave as a polite refusal. Before Mamie Manning could make a decision, the doors closed. Manning clanged the bell once more. Liddell called out the next stop.

Mamie watched as the car continued east in the direction of the lake. If she felt any regret or impending sense of loss, she never spoke of it. She crossed Devon Avenue and stood at the curb waiting for the westbound bus toward home, not realizing that she had seen her husband for the last time.

Chapter
THREE

Around 5:30 p.m., during the heart of the evening rush, Manning and Liddell crossed over the Chicago River, passed under the Lake Street elevated tracks and entered "the Loop," so named for the circuit of "L" tracks created by Lake and Van Buren streets to the north and south, and Wabash and Wells streets to the east and west. Beginning at Lake Street and ending at Van Buren, more passengers would exit and board the trolley than at any other stretch along its entire route. The car was not yet full, and a number of passengers got off to change to the "L" at Lake Street. Others got off in search of entertainment.

At that time, State Street between Lake and Washington boasted a corridor of movie palaces, including the Chicago Theater on the east side of the street and the State/Lake Theater on the opposite side. Marquees that evening offered names like Elizabeth Taylor, Joan Crawford, Van Johnson, Victor Mature, and Abbott & Costello. It was only a Thursday night. The real crowds would come on the weekend and take advantage of the Memorial Day holiday.

Sharing the same corridor and extending several blocks to the south were some of Chicago's largest department stores, including Marshall Field's and Carson, Pirie, Scott's, each offering a different sale for the Memorial Day weekend. Marshall Field's advertised summer apparel, including ladies' hats for the summer at the low price of two dollars. Passenger Mary Kortezynski, 60, had taken advantage of the sale. She was heading home now with a hatbox resting on her lap. The hat inside was pink with flowers on it, and she planned to wear it over the summer.[1]

A few passengers stayed on board the trolley as it entered the Loop. Wilhelmina Hardison, 35, worked at a cleaning and dyeing shop in the northwest suburb of Park Ridge. She was one of Manning and Liddell's first passengers, boarding somewhere along Devon Avenue.[2]

Most of the passengers boarding downtown had no time for shopping. They worked downtown, and they were heading home. Almost all lived on the South Side, and they were a mixture of secretaries, clerks, and elevator operators, domestics, janitors, and others:

* Mary Pokorney, 42, was a Bell Telephone Company supervisor;[3]

* Vernon Anderson worked as an accountant for the *Christian Leader* magazine;[4]

* Eighteen-year-old Arleen Franzen was employed as a page girl at the Illinois Continental Bank downtown;[5]

* Clara Dobson, 31, altered corsets at the Loeber Corset Company located near State and Madison;[6]

* Rosa Saunders, 31, worked downtown as a stock girl at the Chas. A. Stevens company;[7]

* Alean Fisher, 48, was a chambermaid at the Stevens Hotel, before it became the Conrad Hilton.[8]

It was the busiest time of day. Ahead of him on State, Manning could see a line of other trolleys, each taking on passengers and filling their cars. As soon as one car pulled away from a safety island, a dozen other passengers were waiting to board the next car with a dozen more waiting at the next stop. By the time Manning negotiated the eight-block stretch of State Street between Lake and Van Buren streets, most of the seats inside the trolley were filled. A few standees milled about on the rear platform. According to the supervisor on duty, Manning and Liddell left Van Buren at precisely 5:57 p.m.[9]

The trolley continued south, passing through the old Bronzeville neighborhood—a historic district rich in African-American culture and known specifically as a home to jazz and blues clubs during its heyday in the 1920s and '30s. Now the neighborhood was disintegrating. Within a decade, many of the buildings on both sides of State Street would be leveled in favor of the Robert Taylor Homes, a network of 28 apartment buildings, each 16 stories high, which ran for two miles along State Street and came to symbolize the ghetto in Chicago and, indeed, in America for more than four decades.

Near 35th Street, 17-year-old Kyteria Cooper boarded the car. She worked at Spiegel's, a catalog company whose product was known across the country. Instead of going straight home after work, she decided to treat herself to something sweet. At 35th and State, she stopped at a five-and-dime that had a lunch counter. Once there, she selected a dish of strawberry shortcake—the first time she had ever tried the dessert.

Kyteria was born in Mississippi and moved to Chicago with her parents during the great African-American migration of the 1940s. Her parents were barely literate. Her name was intended to have been "Keturah," the name of Abraham's second wife. Her mother wasn't sure how to spell the name, and she became "Kyteria" by default. Her father worked several jobs in Chicago to help make ends meet.[10]

By 43rd Street, more than half the passengers on board were African-American, and the majority of them were headed to the same destination. It was called Princeton Park, and the 36-Broadway/State route ran right alongside its eastern boundary.

Princeton Park was the brainchild of a white real estate developer named Donald O'Toole. It was created in direct response to the mass exodus of African-Americans to Chicago from the South during World War II. Defense jobs were available at that time, particularly in Chicago's steel industry located in the far southeast corner of the city. The problem lay in the lack of housing. Traditionally African-American neighborhoods in Chicago were already overcrowded. There was no place to house prospective African-American workers. Although a northern city, Chicago's neighborhoods were still mostly segregated.

O'Toole managed to convince Mayor Edward Kelly that a housing development created for African-American workers was a worthwhile venture. The selected area was bordered by 91st and 95th streets to the north and south, Wentworth Avenue to the east, and the Chicago & Eastern Illinois Railroad to the west. Throughout the war, 908 houses were planned and built to house between 4,500 and 5,000 people.[11]

The center of the development contained an oval-shaped park complete with a field house and a public school. For a time, Princeton Park became a model community of sorts, with civic organizations, annual lawn and garden contests, and a strong sense of community pride.

If you were a young, working- or middle-class African-American family living on the South Side, Princeton Park was where you wanted to be. The poet Gwendolyn Brooks lived in Princeton Park on Wentworth

Avenue. During the first week of May 1950, Mrs. Brooks became the first African-American to win the Pulitzer Prize.

Kyteria Cooper and her family lived in Princeton Park on 91st Street. Robert Nalls, who worked at a North Side bakery and boarded the car at 47th Street, lived on Wentworth just down the block from Gwendolyn Brooks.

Several other passengers boarding the trolley called Princeton Park home:

At 43rd Street, Mrs. Earl Sue Sharp got on the trolley. She had just left Du Sable High School, where she had volunteered her time as a seamstress sewing costumes for the school's annual "Hi Jinx" variety show. She was headed for her Princeton Park home at 93rd and Stewart streets.[12]

Sixty-five-year-old George Dowdell rode the car with his wife, Bertha. He worked as a Western Union messenger. They lived in Princeton Park as well.[13]

Ora Mae Bryant, 29, lived just a few doors down from Earl Sue Sharp. She boarded at 54th Street after visiting with her mother. Ora Mae was excited and couldn't stop thinking about receiving her diploma from the Madam C. J. Walker College of Beauty and Culture. Her graduation date was fast approaching.[14]

Some passengers were there by chance and were not regular riders. In some cases a slight change in their daily routines placed them on the trolley at that particular time.

Frances Mennite usually came home by another route each day, but on May 25 she left work an hour early to visit her mother, who was ill.[15]

Marie Antoinette Franklin, 41, a special education teacher at Farren Elementary on 50th and Wabash, had been downtown attending a school meeting after regular school hours. She boarded the trolley nearly three hours later than usual.[16]

Nineteen-year-old Carol Rudenga usually took the Rock Island commuter train to her South Side home. Ironically, she worked with Arleen Franzen as a page girl at the same downtown bank. The two exchanged greetings on the trolley but were unable to find seats next to each other.[17]

Carol had just been asked to stand up for her sister's wedding in June and was on her way to 63rd Street and a shopping district that was known for its bargains. She planned to grab a sandwich at a drug store and then hunt for a bridesmaid's dress.[18]

Fifty-ninth Street saw a large turnover in passengers. It was here that State Street passed beneath the Englewood spur of the Jackson

Park/Englewood elevated tracks. Many riders leaving downtown rode the "L" to 59th Street only to transfer to local trolleys that would carry them further south.

Among these new passengers was Martha Mary Jankauskis, 23, a secretary at the Bowman Dairy Company. She seldom rode the trolley at this hour, but she had just put her fur coat in cold storage at a downtown furrier. She wound up about 30 minutes behind her usual schedule.[19]

Fourteen-year-old Beverly Clark was looking forward to a night of youthful freedom. Her parents were out celebrating their wedding anniversary, and Beverly decided to call on a schoolmate. Her friend wasn't home, so she boarded the trolley at 59th Street intent on catching a movie alone. She moved up the aisle and took a seat to the right of Paul Manning at the very front of the car. When an elderly passenger moved through the aisle, Beverly stood up and gave him her seat. She retreated down the aisle and found another seat opposite the center exit vacated by a passenger getting ready to exit at 63rd Street. Her generosity saved her life.[20]

Twenty-five-year-old Eunice Savage was one of the passengers getting ready to disembark. She rose from her seat, negotiated the center aisle, and grabbed the chrome bar in front of the center doors, standing on the treaded step. Like Carol Rudenga, she was on her way to shop on 63rd Street.[21]

Also getting ready to leave was 23-year-old Mildred Thornhill. Sixty-third Street was the end of the line each day for Mildred. She lived in a large tenement at 6241 S. State, which formed the southern boundary of the turnaround loop at 62nd Place. On most days, she exited the trolley at the safety island just down the block near 63rd Street. She crossed to the east side of the street and walked north past a few storefronts to her building. She had no way of knowing it, but this evening's trolley was about to deposit her at her front doorstep.[22]

After the busy intersection at 59th and State, William Liddell resumed his conversation with a passenger-acquaintance named John Seawright, who had boarded the trolley at 46th Street. They were so deeply engrossed in their conversation that Seawright forgot to call for his regular stop at 61st Street just a few blocks from his home at 6194 South Park Avenue. He remained on the car, content to exit at 63rd Street. Had Seawright exited at his customary stop, it might have delayed the trolley's arrival at the turnaround by several crucial seconds.[23]

No passengers claimed to have boarded at 61st Street, and there is considerable evidence from motorists that the trolley never stopped there. The sun, though setting, was still quite high in the sky and had not yet ducked behind the buildings along the west side of State Street. From the perspective of the southbound trolley, the sun shone to the right and slightly behind motorman Paul Manning, sometimes visible in the windshields of parked or passing cars.

Liddell could feel the sunlight through the windows of the car as he turned to face boarding passengers. His view of the front of the car was obscured by passengers standing in the aisle. He continued to talk to Seawright, but he prepared himself for 63rd Street, which would be another major intersection as passengers departed for home and for the shopping district. As he passed a gasoline station on the east side of State, Liddell instinctively reached up and grabbed a chrome handrail, bracing himself for the deceleration of the car as it neared the safety island located just north of the busy intersection and the underpass.

Instead, Liddell became aware of a familiar but unexpected sound— the buzzing emitted when the car's emergency brake was applied. Before he knew what had happened, Liddell began to slide from his seat. In an instant, he was on the floor.[24]

Just after 6:30 p.m., Charles Kleim continued to stand in front of the switch. He was tired but invigorated with the hope that his long day was nearly over. The Streets and Sanitation crew had nearly emptied the viaduct at 63rd and State, and the news was relayed to the supervisor in the turnaround that trolley traffic could resume in as few as 10 or 15 minutes.[25]

To that point, Kleim had been on the job for nearly 15 hours. He watched a southbound trolley approach at 62nd Street and flagged it to a stop in front of the switch. Inside, motorman George Hartwig eased his trolley into the turnaround and traveled the circumference of the loop to a point where the supervisor waited to give him further instructions.

Almost immediately after Hartwig's trolley entered the loop, Kleim spotted another trolley approaching. As he had done more than 200 times that afternoon, he began waving as the trolley entered the 6200 block of State Street—an obvious waving of the arms intended to get the attention of the motorman.

But as the trolley neared the switch, it became obvious to Kleim that the motorman was not responding to his signals. The trolley continued to approach at an alarming speed. He began to wave more intently, gesturing with palms down as if to say, "Easy does it, buddy! Back off!" From his perspective, the motorman was seated upright and looking straight ahead. Kleim grew agitated. He took a step or two toward the oncoming car, trying one final, frantic wave. The car seemed to slow somewhat, but it was still traveling far too fast to make the switch. As he ducked to his left and out of the trolley's path, Kleim first heard the trolley as it lurched into the switch, followed by the telltale crunch of metal on metal. Seconds later, the first screams began.[26]

Vehicular traffic through the flooded underpass had resumed in the late afternoon due in large part to the pumping efforts of the Streets and Sanitation crews. As Manning's trolley left 59th Street and neared the turnaround, the motorman could see southbound automobiles and trucks entering the underpass ahead of him, and northbound vehicles emerging from the opposite lane.

Approaching in the northbound lane was a Mack A Model truck tractor with a double-bottom rig, hauling two fuel tanks loaded with 4,000 gallons of gasoline apiece. The driver, Mel Wilson, 39, was an employee of Sprout & Davis, a gasoline distributor out of Whiting, Indiana, who had a lease with Standard Oil. Wilson had been employed by Sprout & Davis for several years and had a flawless safety record. He was married and lived in Valparaiso, Indiana, with his wife and four children.[27]

Wilson left Whiting after the rains had already come and gone. In the days before expressways, he slogged his way down major thoroughfares during the peak hours of traffic congestion. With few ordinances regulating gasoline haulage in the city, Wilson drove his truck along the busiest thoroughfares. Since his truck was based outside of the city, neither of the tanks he hauled was compartmented. As he drove his truck through the receding waters of the underpass, Wilson had yet to make his first delivery of the day.

Emerging from the underpass in the northbound lane, Wilson could have seen George Hartwig's Green Hornet passing across his own lane and into the turnaround loop. As his truck slowly climbed the incline of the grade coming out of the underpass, he might have noticed Charles Kleim as he tried to wave down Manning's streetcar. His attention would most likely have been on the traffic in front of him. As he drew parallel to the turnaround, Mel Wilson probably didn't even know what hit him.

Directly opposite the entrance to the turnaround stood the only house on the west side of the street—6242 S. State Street, which belonged to Walter Skonicki, a 48-year-old maintenance engineer for the Chicago Board of Education. Like Charles Kleim, Skonicki shared his home with his wife and older children ranging in age from 15 to 23 years. The evening meal was just concluding.[28]

The Skonicki house was one of the oldest in the neighborhood, probably predating 1889 when Chicago annexed the bustling village of Englewood and transformed it from a "streetcar suburb" into another intricate piece in the city's expanding South Side. Where bungalows and two-story frame houses now dotted neighboring streets, the Skonicki house was reminiscent of a clapboard farmhouse with a rustic character all its own. Local lore suggested that it had once served as Englewood's first post office. Over the years, various additions—some haphazard in appearance—had been made to the original structure.

Just before 6:30 p.m., Skonicki ambled into the living room and, as part of his evening ritual, deposited himself on the sofa. Television was still an expensive novelty. Instead, Skonicki might have listened to the radio or thumbed his way through the evening edition of one of Chicago's four daily papers. Looking out through two large front windows past a low porch and across the sidewalk, he had a bird's-eye view of the entrance to the turnaround loop. The afternoon rains had dropped the temperature to a cool 64 degrees. The living room windows were wide open, as were many windows throughout the house, and they drew in the first comfortable air of the week.

Skonicki looked out the window and watched as the evening rush hour wound down. Traffic and its many sounds gradually abated. In the grassy area within the turnaround, a small group of boys tossed a grimy tennis ball near a tumbledown wooden fence that ran adjacent to the CTA supervisor's shack. Commuters returned home to the large, three-story tenement at 6241 S. State, which faced the Skonicki home. The first few evening patrons entered the tavern located on the ground floor of the tenement. A large ad for Atlas-Prager Beer was painted on the north wall of the building. There was moderate foot traffic along the network of "mom and pop" shops and apartments leading down to the corner at 63rd Street.

Skonicki's attention wandered to Charles Kleim standing in front of the switch in the middle of the street. Flaggers were a frequent sight at the turnaround loop, although Skonicki thought it strange that this one had no flags. He watched as the big man waved to an unseen trolley approaching from the north. He heard it as it rumbled to a halt in front of Kleim and watched as George Hartwig carefully guided his vehicle across the northbound lanes of traffic and into the alleyway entrance of the turnaround.

A moment later, when he glanced again at the middle of the street, Skonicki noted that Kleim was no longer in front of the switch. In fact, Skonicki saw him standing on the sidewalk across the street from his house talking to a supervisor—the second instance of odd behavior on the part of the flagger that resonated with Skonicki.[29]

Skonicki briefly averted his eyes. Within seconds, he heard the sound of a terrific collision on the street in front of him, followed immediately by a rush of air through the front windows that blew the sofa on which he lay several feet backwards. "What the heck?!" He sprang from the couch and ran to the window. He couldn't believe what he saw. It looked like the whole street had been firebombed. Skonicki tore himself away from the view and ran for the phone in the kitchen.

Seated at the controls of the trolley, Paul Manning was visible only to those passengers at the front of the car. During the last moments of his life, no passenger reported anything out of the ordinary regarding Manning's appearance or demeanor. He did not seem to have been stricken physically. He was upright and alert and did not appear to be distracted.[30]

It is impossible to know what was going through Manning's mind as the trolley came abreast of the turnaround at 62nd Place. Cars and trucks passing through the viaduct ahead of him may have led him to believe that he, too, would continue south through the tunnel. He gave no indication that he saw Charles Kleim imploring him to slow down at the switch ahead.

Whatever his state of mind or rationale, Manning realized his mistake too late.

At least one passenger reported that Manning slapped down on an emergency brake handle just prior to the collision, which corresponded with the "buzzing" sound heard by William Liddell just before the crash. Several recalled hearing him cry out, then throw up his hands.[31]

The trolley careened violently as it entered the switch. Before anyone had any idea what was happening, the 20-ton vehicle broadsided Mel Wilson's cab at the driver's side door. The impact flattened one of the truck's own gas tanks, causing an immediate explosion. All at once, a ball of fire shot through the trolley's shattered windshield and tore through the interior of the car. The semitrailer unhitched and continued to roll forward. As it did so, a ten-inch gash was ripped in the skin of the tank it was hauling. Gasoline began to pour from the hole. With a fire raging just a few feet away, the fuel had an immediate ignition source.[32]

The collision caused the rear wheels of the trolley to derail and then skid sideways for several feet. The four-ton steel wheels left deep gouges in the asphalt street below. For one heart-stopping moment, the car tipped dangerously to the right before righting itself and landing on its wheels. Had the car rolled over, all of its doors would have been rendered useless. As it turned out, the utility of the doors was about to be tested.[33]

With no time to recover from the collision, the passengers began a helter-skelter scramble away from the flames and toward the rear of the car. It lay nearly perpendicular to State Street, as if placed there as a police barricade. Only about ten feet separated the trolley and the gas truck. Flaming gasoline ran over the curb and sidewalk, setting fire to the tenement at 6241 S. State. Following the path of least resistance, it ran in the gaps between the rails and brick pavers that reinforced the rails on either side. It followed the grade of the street and quickly set fire to cars parked on the east side of the street.

In a matter of seconds, flaming gasoline had completely enveloped the trolley.

At the center of the car, Beverly Clark was knocked to the floor. Flames from the initial explosion made it impossible to exit through the double doors at the front of the car adjacent to Paul Manning. Passengers who somehow survived the shower of glass and flames now stampeded toward the rear.

Some of them stepped on Beverly, who managed to right herself and cross the crowded aisle, slamming into the center door with her shoulder. It wouldn't open. Then Beverly remembered a childhood prank that saved her life. She reached above her head and felt for the emergency door release.

"I knew where it was because when we kids went to school, we used to pull it just for fun to (heckle) the conductor and the motorman."[34]

Her fingers found the lever and she pulled. The door opened suddenly, and Beverly tumbled to the pavement. Several other passengers followed her to safety before the flames from the gas-fed fire grew more intense and beat the others back toward the rear platform.

"The people were all in flames and screaming. Before I fell out, the last thing I saw was the old man I'd given my seat to. He was covered with blood. When I got out, I started to run. I ran into a boy I knew at school and he thought I was crazy because I couldn't talk."[35]

In shock from her ordeal, Beverly continued to run until she was stopped by two policewomen who were writing parking tickets near the scene. They took her to St. Bernard Hospital where she was treated for contusions to her head and for a broken finger that she sustained during the initial commotion within the car.

In the chaos on the rear platform, William Liddell tried to get to his feet. Several passengers stepped on his back as they fought their way to the rear doors. The fire began to consume the leather upholstery and rubber floor mats. Smoke grew thick and noxious, making breathing difficult and contributing to the mounting panic and confusion. Through the windows on either side of the vehicle, passengers saw only flames. It was a disorienting sensation. Where to go? The rear doors and windows seemed the most likely route to daylight, but the growing fire seemed to surround even those potential exits.

Liddell managed to pull himself into his conductor's seat where he could set the levers to open the rear doors. At that moment, several passengers were trying to force open the doors. Edward White, who had been seated directly opposite Liddell, tried kicking the door. He managed to break a glass window pane in one of the lower panels, injuring his right leg in the process.[36] Beside him, John Seawright pulled at the rubber inserts between the doors, trying to get them to swivel open.[37] Neither was successful. Other passengers crowded and pushed behind White and Seawright, making it difficult for either man to maintain his balance.

What happened next was a fantastic stroke of luck. At his seat, Liddell managed to set the levers to open. Had Edward White, John Seawright, or any other passenger on the rear platform exerted pressure on the doors at that moment, it is unlikely that they would have opened. Passengers may have responded to Liddell's cries to stand clear of the doors. With no pressure pushing outward, all three doors opened inward. Edward White toppled to the ground and limped to the curb on the opposite side of State Street. His clothing was already singed, and a passerby threw her coat over his shoulders. Seawright landed on his feet and had the presence of mind to grab two other passengers—likely Mary Pokorney and Eunice Savage—and pull them through the open doors. Again, several other passengers followed them to safety.[38]

But the crush of passengers was too intense. By now, more than 60 passengers were tightly wedged in front of the doors, in the aisle, and on the seats that ran around the platform. Clothing began to catch fire. Women's hair began to burn.

People toppled through, and then into the open doors, some catching their arms, shoulders, and clothing in the door panels. The doors could not withstand the pressure exerted against them. With safety just inches away, the doors were forced shut. Amid cries of despair, passengers scratched, clawed, and kicked at the panels, pulling at the inserts as Seawright had done before. Liddell yelled as loudly as he could. "Stand back from the doors! They'll open, just stand back!"

But the mob moved as one now. The crush of humanity made movement almost impossible. Pressure exerted on passengers caused bones to break and made breathing impossible. The heat was unbearable. There was no air and, it seemed, no place to go. Some passengers lost consciousness even before the flames reached them.

Those caught at the back of the pile saw the futility of a door exit and looked for another route. Although accounts vary as to whom and how, someone had the presence of mind to break the two rear windows. Passengers immediately began to pour out.

Max Weinstein, a 62-year-old tailor on his way to dinner at his son's house, saw his chance.

"I was lucky, because I had been standing near the conductor and had happened to get a seat near him. When the crash occurred, I thought I'd never get out. I fell down and the people trampled on me at first. Then I managed to get up. The fire was already in the streetcar. I saw a man break a rear window with his shoe and plunge out the window. I had to dive out the window head first. I was the fifth one who jumped out. I got all scratched up and my hair is singed."[39]

But it was better than the alternative. Others followed Weinstein through the rear window in a disorderly effort to escape. To exit through the window, passengers climbed on rear seats and crawled through the opening. Although one window was always bolted shut, its twin should have opened freely, greatly expediting the escape rate. But in the chaos on the rear platform, no one thought to unlatch the window. Although the opening was 27 inches wide, the metal bar that ran horizontally across the middle of the pane reduced the height to just under 13 inches. By breaking the window, passengers reduced their egress to one-half its size. The windows should have meant salvation for many more people. Instead, they became another logjam.

Most passengers who made it through dove headfirst like Weinstein or were shoved through by the persons behind them. Many hit the ground hard, often with one or more passengers landing on top of them. Civilians brave enough to approach the blaze helped pull survivors from the window and help them to a safer location. But after the first 10 or 15 got out, even the most stalwart of Samaritans was beaten back by the heat as the fire continued to grow. Those left inside were on their own.

Arleen Franzen lost her shoes in the dash to the rear of the car. By the time she got there, she could see there was no hope in exiting through the doors. She decided to try to climb out of one of the rear windows. Arleen was a slender girl, but it was going to be a tight squeeze. She climbed onto a seat, turned her head sideways, and started through the opening.

"People were crowding against the doors and I could see there was no sense in trying to get out there. I saw some people trying to get out of (rear) windows and I tried to get out that way, too. I was hanging half way out the window, but I couldn't make it the rest of the way."[40]

Franzen dangled from the window for what seemed like an eternity until someone pulled her to safety.

Kyteria Cooper was one of the few passengers who wasn't knocked to the floor at the time of the collision. Seated two seats from the rear doors on the right-hand side, she grabbed the grip bar of the seat ahead of her as the car swerved into the switch.

"I got up and headed toward the door, but I saw that the people couldn't get out. Then I saw that someone broke the back window. I had caught on fire. Practically all my hair on the left-hand side had burned off. And my clothes. I fell out the back window and I ran up on the railroad tracks."[41]

From the railroad embankment that ran diagonally across State Street and behind the Skonicki house, Kyteria looked out over the inferno that had moments before been a normal city block at the end of the work day.

"And all I saw—God—was the big fire. The balls that were going up in the air."[42]

As the first explosion tore its way through the interior of the trolley, Charles Kleim retreated to what he sensed was a safe distance from the blast, waiting to see if another, more powerful explosion was about to follow. When it appeared that the gas tanks were not about to erupt in a pyrotechnic display, he ran back to the car.

Using a wooden pole attached to the roof of the vehicle, he swiveled the trolley pole sideways, breaking contact between the trolley wheel and the electric power source above the street. He then directed his attention to the rear window where he began to help pull passengers through the narrow space between the bars.[43] One of the passengers he aided was Arleen Franzen, who had gotten stuck as she shimmied her way through the opening. The bottoms of her feet were burned, but she ran into the lot adjacent to the Skonicki house. She did not run as far as the railroad embankment, but turned and watched the blaze. At the rear of the car, she saw her co-worker, Carol Rudenga:

"I saw Caroline hanging by the waist from the same window I escaped through. She was trying to get out, but she couldn't make it. Then the flames caught fire to her hair and I saw her sink back down inside the car."[44]

Still parked in the turnaround less than 50 yards from the wreckage, passengers on board George Hartwig's trolley stared in disbelief. Carol Peterson was a 20-year-old secretary on her way home, thankful that she had caught Hartwig's trolley and not the one that followed it:

"Everyone on my car seemed to catch their breath when the car hit the trailer truck. When it burst into flames, folks rushed from our car. Everyone was running around in the other car by then, screaming horribly. I saw two people break out windows in the back of the car."[45]

Hartwig decided that the turnaround might not be the safest place to be: "Flaming gasoline was rolling down the street, so I got my passengers out of my car."[46]

Hartwig was able to see into the front of the trolley where Paul Manning, apparently pinned in the wreck, struggled within the flames.

"I turned my head," Hartwig said. "I couldn't stand it. I saw enough of that in the service."[47]

Sitting behind the wheel of his car in the filling station across the street, Rev. R. J. Sidney watched as the catastrophe erupted before him. Sidney, a visiting minister at South Shore Baptist Church, had just purchased gas at the station and was about to pull into traffic on State Street when the accident occurred. He heard the screams and pleas of mercy as passengers fought to escape. He smelled the burning gasoline, but he could also smell the odor of burnt flesh. He watched as shadows struggled within the trolley, writhing in agony, until they collapsed and disappeared from view.

Sidney also witnessed several passengers exit through the rear windows. Then, when it seemed that the flames were too thick and no one else could escape them, he saw Alma Featherstone at the opening. Featherstone's hair and clothes were ablaze, and as Arleen Franzen and Carol Rudenga had done, she dangled by the waist from the window.

Unable to go to her aid, Rev. Sidney offered a prayer on her behalf: "I may have asked in an ignorant way, but I said, 'God, will you let her come out?'"[48]

Alma Featherstone crumpled to the pavement. A courageous onlooker risked personal injury by rushing to Featherstone's side, smothering her burning clothing and dragging her to safety.

Ambulances had yet to arrive at the scene. Rev. Sidney took Featherstone and passengers Vernon Anderson and Ben Head into his car. On the drive to the hospital, Featherstone, still conscious, asked Sidney, "Reverend, how do I look?"[49]

Sidney didn't know what to say. Featherstone had third-degree burns over every exposed part of her body, including her face and hands. "Never mind that, child," he said. "We're going to get you some help."

Alma Featherstone was the last passenger to escape from the trolley.

When she fell from the rear window, less than four minutes had elapsed since the collision. Within another 60 seconds, the trolley's outline was no longer visible within the flames. As the fire in the tenement raged, one had the perception that the entire block was on fire.

Inside the car, the fire continued its devastation. With plenty of oxygen and a near-constant supply of fuel, it consumed everything that could burn. Seats, floor mats, insulation, wires. The fire reduced the interior to a shell. Even the sheet metal exterior buckled under the intense heat, giving the once streamlined vehicle the look of a badly treated aluminum can. For passengers who were unable to exit, the trolley became a crematory.

The first fire crews began to arrive within minutes of the collision. With flames towering several stories over the street, most had no idea that a streetcar was involved in the fire.

Lasker's first photo shows a moment of chaos on State St. about ten minutes after the collision. Fire continues to shoot from the gasoline truck, which is lost in the smoke and flames. (Courtesy of Stephen Lasker)

Quickly overwhelmed by the blaze, firefighters enlisted civilians who temporarily helped man the hoses. (Courtesy of Stephen Lasker)

More than 100 people were left homeless in the fire, which completely destroyed the tenement shown here. The gasoline truck is partially visible on the sidewalk, but the trolley is hidden behind thick smoke. (Courtesy of Stephen Lasker)

Smoke drew Southsiders to the blaze in droves. By the time the fires were extinguished, more than 15,000 had packed the area. (Courtesy of Stephen Lasker)

(left) Inches from safety. Lasker's photo of the charred remains of passengers piled in front of exit doors caused a shudder throughout the city and called into question the safety of the vehicles. (Courtesy of Stephen Lasker)

(below) Grim-faced firefighters carry the fragile remains of a victim away from the trolley. (Courtesy of Stephen Lasker)

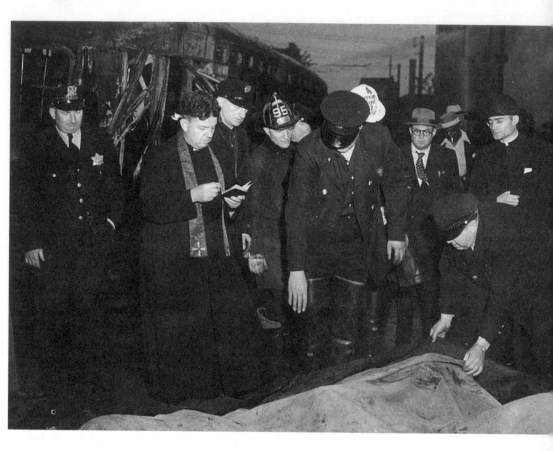

(left) A fire department chaplain administers the last rites to 33 victims whose bodies were covered with a canvas tarpaulin. (Courtesy of Stephen Lasker)

(below) A hive of activity on State Street. A temporary morgue is established on the sidewalk just steps away from the ruined shell of the trolley. (Courtesy of the Chicago Transit Authority)

(left) Firefighters manage to extinguish the gasoline fire and wash excess fuel down a nearby sewer drain. (Courtesy of the Chicago Transit Authority)

(below) The truck tractor and the tankers were hauled into the turnaround entrance after the truck fire was extinguished. Note that the trolley has been returned to the tracks. (Courtesy of the Chicago Transit Authority)

(above) More than 200 firefighters and 30 pieces of equipment were used to fight the fire, which caused damage to seven buildings on the east side of State Street. (Courtesy of Stephen Lasker)

(right) The trolley broadsided the truck at the driver's side door. The initial explosion came when the impact flattened the truck's own supply tank (right foreground). Driver Mel Wilson's lunchbox lies just to the left. (Courtesy of the Chicago Transit Authority)

(right) The battered watch by which Paul Manning's body was identified. Police used the watch to establish the exact time of the accident. (Courtesy of Michael R. Medley)

(below) Northbound view of the switch at the entrance to the turnaround one day after the accident. Note the deep gouges in the pavement (left center) caused when the trolley derailed after colliding with the truck. (Courtesy of the Chicago Transit Authority)

(*left*) Charles Kleim, who was the flagger at the scene of the accident, circa 1941. (Courtesy of Douglas J. Kleim)

(*below*) Paul Manning in his CTA motorman's uniform during the winter of 1950, just months before the accident that would end his life. (Courtesy of Michael R. Medley)

Chapter
FOUR

Electricity and phone service on the east side of State Street was knocked out within the first few minutes after the collision. The first call for help may have come from Walter Skonicki's kitchen just moments after the crash.

Before an official alarm went out, firefighters from a nearby station responded. Fireman Martin Mulhall was standing in front of his station at 6017 S. State, just two blocks from the scene. Mulhall heard the explosion and saw thick, black smoke billowing across State Street.

"Let's go!" he hollered. "We've got a fire down the street!"[1]

In a breach of department protocol, Lt. Edward Fitzgerald did not wait for an official alarm from downtown, but ordered a truck down State Street. They were the first crew at the scene, arriving not long after Alma Featherstone escaped from the trolley.

Fitzgerald and his men were faced with a chaos unlike any they had ever faced or prepared for. Mulhall jumped off the truck and saw a man standing on the side of the street with his clothes on fire. He knocked the man to the ground and rolled him around until the flames were extinguished. Then he took a look around.

"Flames were shooting 250 feet into the air. There was fire everywhere, on the street, in passing autos and in the buildings on both sides of State Street."[2]

Immediately after arriving at the scene, Fitzgerald put Emergency Plan No. 4 into effect, which called for all available police, ambulance crews, and rescue squads.[3]

Fitzgerald sent part of his crew into the tenement and adjacent buildings to clear them of any residents. The rest manned hoses and tried to get water on the burning tenement. The front of the building was completely ablaze, from the street level to the roof. While one firefighter trained his hose on the front of the building, another lugged a hose into the turnaround. A hole was hacked through the wooden fence near the entrance to the turnaround, and a firefighter dragged a line onto the trolley tracks adjacent to the building.

After water was thrown onto the front of the building, the fire receded enough to reveal the epicenter of the blaze. The trolley was still burning but its silhouette was partially visible. Flames continued to shoot out from beneath the ruptured gas tank as if someone had placed a lighter in front of an aerosol spray. Fireballs erupted one after another and rose into the air.

"We couldn't see anything but a great sea of flame," one firefighter remembered. "We turned one hose on the nearby buildings and the other in the general direction of the accident. It was the worst fire I've seen in 13 years as a city fireman."[4]

Employing a "fog mantle" spray nozzle—a technique a number of firefighters learned battling oil fires in World War II—firefighters sprayed a fine mist over the ruptured gas tank and gradually suffocated the fire. Once it was extinguished, they washed the remaining gasoline from the first tank into a nearby sewer.[5]

But as the gas fire was being extinguished, the tenement fire continued to rage out of control, spreading to adjacent buildings on the east side of State. Firefighters had quickly cleared the tenement and four nearby buildings of all occupants. A secondary explosion was averted when fire crews pumped water into a fuel tank located adjacent to one of the burning buildings. A strong wind from the north blew flaming debris onto the rooftops of the smaller buildings to the south. Within a short time, five buildings were in flames. The fire was upgraded to a four-alarm. A total of more than 30 fire trucks and engines were called to the scene.[6]

Nineteen-year-old Steve Lasker worked part-time at his father's Hyde Park cleaners, but he aspired to make photography his full-time gig. As a teenager, he attached himself to a local firehouse at 46th Street and Cottage Grove, about six blocks from the family business. Lasker started hanging out at the station after school, helping out wherever he could. What really made him one of the boys was when he began to take photos of the firefighters, their families, first communions, softball games, etc.—all for free.

In exchange, Lasker convinced the firemen to take him out on calls. He brought along his miniature Speed Graphic camera, snapping fire photos, which he gave to the firemen and occasionally sold to local newspapers, including *The Hyde Park Herald* in his own neighborhood.

Short in stature, he became a sort of firehouse mascot. He was given his own hat, coat, boots, and bunk. He learned which pieces of equipment were called for as blazes were upgraded from one-alarm to two-alarm, etc. He also learned the venerable joker system which, like an old telegraph, tapped out the locations of fires.

As he spent more and more time at the station, a sort of symbiotic relationship formed between Lasker's family and the firehouse. His father cleaned the firefighters' clothes for free. His mother sewed their buttons and cuffs. Lasker continued to learn his craft and develop his eye.

On the day of the accident, he worked at the cleaners until 5:00 p.m. and then borrowed his father's car to drive to the station.

He was in the firehouse at about 6:40 p.m. when the initial straight box alarm came in, likely originating from a pulled fire alarm box near the scene of the accident. The joker clicked out the location. The alarm called for four engines, two trucks, and a battalion chief.

"(Our) engine and the hook-and-ladder weren't due until the second alarm, but the Chief had to go because the 11th Battalion Chief was out on another call.

"So the Chief said to me, 'We've got some kind of streetcar on fire. You'll have to get in the back here.'

"Now, (the chiefs) drove coupes. They didn't have four-doors. I just took my camera and pack and threw it in the back. I almost laid across it because of all the helmets, coats, and boots."[7]

In his bag, Lasker had his Speed Graphic and about eight film slides.

"It was one shot per side of the holder. You had to take it out, turn it over, put the slide in and cock the shutter. It was very slow, but it was the best thing out there for newspaper style photography."[8]

Lasker pulled on his gear as the chief wove his way through traffic.

"The Chief took Cottage Grove into Washington Park and Garfield Boulevard to State Street. And as we turned onto State, you could see the black smoke coming up, but you couldn't tell what it was yet. As we pulled up, we could see the streetcar was sideways."[9]

The chief pulled as close to the wreckage as he dared, careful to leave room for other fire equipment. Lasker, dressed now in his firefighter gear, stood in the middle of State Street and grabbed a quick shot to establish the scene.

Taken from a distance of about 100 feet, the photo showed a moment of disarray and confusion on State Street probably less than 15 minutes after the accident. The trolley, still partially shrouded in smoke and flames, lay perpendicular to the street. The gasoline truck and front of the tenement were completely engulfed in flames. Curious onlookers crossed State Street at all angles, and several ventured to within 20 feet of the trolley. A growing crowd had gathered on the sidewalk in front of the turnaround near the burning shell of an automobile parked at the curb. Several hose lines had already been run, but only one hose, trained on a side window of the tenement, was functioning.

Flaming gasoline ran in rivulets in the ruts of the street where the trolley tracks lay. An older man in overalls carried a load of sand to dump on the hoses where they crossed the flaming tracks. Police had not yet arrived.

Lasker grabbed two more shots as firefighters, aided by bystanders, trained the first hose on the gas truck. He then crossed the street to get a broader view of the tenement fire and the efforts of firefighters to control the gas fire. When it was safe to approach the trolley, he cut around the back of the vehicle to the right side. Firefighters from Rescue Squads 3, 5, and 12 were already there, and using pry bars, they peeled away the panels of the rear blinker doors until they opened and fanned outward. A group of firemen was gathered around the door. Lasker waited for the group to part and then stepped forward. He gazed at the smoldering interior of the car, not yet able to make sense of what was before him.

"I walked around to the back side, and I saw this streetcar with all this stuff in it. And I say 'stuff' because I didn't know what it was. One of the firemen from the Squad 3 said, 'Steve, those are bodies.' Well, I got sick to my stomach. And I don't know what else I did except set up as quickly as I could and shot a picture of it."[10]

Within a decade, Lasker would be one of Chicago's best news photographers—a Pulitzer Prize candidate who seemed to be at every major Chicago news story. But at that moment, he was still an amateur, and he had never taken a photo like this one before.

Lasker set up just to the left of the blinker doors and clicked his shutter. Nearly 60 years after it was taken, it is difficult for the viewer to reconcile what the photo depicts: A firefighter walks out of the picture to the right. The door panels, still connected at the top, are twisted and spread outward like an upside-down fan.

At first glance, the doorway seems to be filled with a material resembling burned cotton batting. It is hard to find any semblance of humanity in the mass—to distinguish form from lifeless form. It is as if all the featureless figures discovered in the ruins of Pompeii had been fused together in a single, ghastly sculpture. Then a shoulder appears. A foot. A torso, bent backwards. A head. Another.

The haunting image taken by Lasker might be considered too graphic by today's standards. But in 1950 Chicago, it appeared on the evening news and was published in several of the city's daily papers. With a click of his shutter, Lasker gave Chicagoans a concrete image that told a more vivid story than any newspaper article ever could. Those who dared could imagine themselves or a loved one among the tangled, grizzly remains. They could wrap their brains around the chaos and terror at the rear doors in the passengers' final moments. The image caused a shudder throughout Chicago.

Lasker took several more shots of the fire as it gutted the buildings on the east side of the street. It was just after 7:00 p.m., and it was still light outside. Most of the fire crews had arrived, and they were doing their best to contain the blaze.

A vacant lot in the middle of the block acted as a temporary fire wall, but the strong winds caused flaming debris to set fire to the remaining structures all the way to the corner of 63rd and State streets. In all, seven buildings caught fire, and five of them were completely destroyed. Miraculously, no injuries were reported in the buildings, although an estimated 120 people were left homeless. The Red Cross was called in to care for the displaced, most of whom lost everything they owned. Temporary shelters were set up at two locations in the area.[11]

Shortly after the gas fire was extinguished and the unburned fuel was drained and washed into the sewers, efforts were made to move the truck tractor and trailers to a safer, temporary location. The second trailer was undamaged in the collision. Its tank had been exposed to extreme heat as the contents of its counterpart burned. But the vents within the tank functioned properly and the cargo of 4,000 additional gallons of gasoline never caught fire.[12]

With its first effort, a city tow truck tore the front bumper from the truck. Then, by rigging a makeshift hitch, the tow truck managed to pull Mel Wilson's truck out from under the semitrailer containing the damaged tank. It was slow going, as all of the Mack's tires had melted down to the rims. The trolley had pulverized the truck tractor, nearly shearing the cab from its frame. Viewed head-on, the cab leaned as if it might tumble upon itself like a house of cards. The roof of the cab was torn away and crumpled accordion-style. The frame was bent. Mel Wilson never had a chance.

The tow truck eventually hauled the truck into the alleyway entrance of the turnaround about 30 feet from the street. The semitrailer and second trailer were deposited adjacent to the truck, still relatively close to the tenement fire, which was starting to burn itself out. The downslope toward the street made it easier for firefighters to wash away the gasoline from the second tank, which was drained when the tenement fire was finally extinguished.

As crews removed the gas truck from the street, about 18 firefighters from the three rescue squads set up a temporary morgue on the broad sidewalk directly in front of the Skonicki home. Two police "squadrols"—a new hybrid of squad car and patrol wagon that was soon dubbed a "paddy wagon"—were pulled onto the sidewalk about 60 feet apart to help cordon off the area and dissuade pedestrian traffic. Between them, firefighters lay two enormous canvas tarpaulins, each folded in half to cover the sidewalk and shroud the remains of the victims as they were brought from the trolley's interior.

Recovery of the remains began soon after. No firefighter at the scene had ever experienced this kind of recovery.

"I've seen burned bodies before," said Arthur Pansegrau, captain of Rescue Squad 12, "but never piled up and burned in a mass like that."[13]

"The only thing I've seen that comes close to it is when we took over a Nazi crematorium during the war," remarked a World War II veteran in the crowd.[14]

It was silent, somber business. Firefighters worked quickly but as respectfully as they could. They did their best to ignore the overwhelming stench of charred flesh. They somehow composed themselves when, in the delicate process of separating bodies, a brittle limb became separated from its owner.

One by one, each body was placed atop a small canvas tarp and borne away by five or six firefighters, and then was carefully removed and placed on the larger tarpaulin on the sidewalk. Mel Wilson's body was the first, pulled from the cab of his truck and kept separate from the rest for the purpose of identification. It took nearly an hour before the last remains were recovered.

Steve Lasker's final few shots focused on the firefighters as they bore the remains along the short distance between the trolley and the sidewalk. Their expressions are pained, like men standing on either side of a much heavier object. The effort evident on their faces was psychological, not physical. Recovery was sometimes a part of the job on a rescue squad. By the time they arrived at the scene, there had been no one to rescue. Death had come too swiftly.

In separating and transporting the bodies to the sidewalk morgue, great care was taken with respect to personal items found among the dead. Since the flames had made identification of many of the victims a near impossibility, even the most trivial of objects found on a set of remains might aid in the identification process later on.

Among these were jewelry, unburned remnants of clothing, shoes, wallets, purses, compacts, glasses.[15]

Several Catholic priests were allowed to cross the police line to deliver the last rites of the Catholic Church. Most prominent among them was Msgr. William Gorman, Fire Department chaplain. Gorman had made headlines three years earlier when he agreed to preside over the burial of Al Capone. Now he and several colleagues stood over the tarpaulins in full-length cassocks, bookended by Fire Department brass and firefighters from the rescue squads who had just finished recovering the bodies from the wrecked streetcar. All heads were bowed, with helmets and hats removed. Facial expressions were sorrowful, some still showing signs of disbelief. [16]

Before he left, Lasker was approached by some news reporters who heard he had been the first photographer at the scene.

"Who do you work for?" one asked him.

"I'm freelance," Lasker said.

"Well, if you can get your pictures to the Merchandise Mart before ten o'clock, we'll use them on the news tonight. There's a hundred bucks in it for you."[17]

Lasker asked a firefighter to drive him back to the station. Before getting in the car, he turned and clicked his shutter one last time. The street was congested with fire trucks, ambulances, squadrols, and other emergency vehicles. Fire hoses stretched for the length of a city block and crisscrossed the wide thoroughfare. Smoke still hung over State Street like a pall, but it was not as dark and thick as before.

As he drove home, he imagined that his father had to walk home that night, and he probably wasn't in the best of moods because of it. Lasker didn't mind. For once he had a good excuse.

Meanwhile, the CTA dispatched utility vehicles to the scene with a re-covery crew of its own. The crew of a CTA tower truck equipped with a pulley managed to raise the rear wheels of the trolley and restore them to the tracks. While the structural fires still burned, the battered hulk of trolley No. 7078 was towed slowly north on State Street. The vehicles made a left-hand turn at 59th Street and then another at Wentworth. With darkness approaching, the trolley passed 6143 S. Wentworth—the home of Beverly Clark. Beverly was still receiving treatment for her injuries and was not yet home to witness the passing of the vehicle. But family and friends who saw it stood slack-jawed in wonder. How could anyone survive such a thing?

The injured were taken to four different area hospitals. Most were transported by ambulance or police car, but several were taken by motorists who happened to be in the vicinity and volunteered their vehicles.

Located just four blocks from the accident scene, St. Bernard Hospital received the most survivors. Day-shift doctors, nurses, and orderlies had already gone home for the day. A smaller night crew was settling in when the first ambulances arrived shortly before 7 p.m. Within minutes, the lobby was filled with injured people, some moaning with broken bones and bruises, other suffering from severe burns and smoke inhalation. As he helped one survivor into the building, a police officer called out to an orderly, "There must be a hundred more up the street! A streetcar just hit a gasoline truck!"[18]

The staff remained calm. Hospital supervisor Sister Mary Immaculata recalled all physicians, nurses, med students, and interns back to duty. A triage was organized to determine those patients in most critical need of treatment. By 7:30 p.m., at least 20 survivors had been taken to St. Bernard's. About half were treated for superficial injuries including cuts, bruises, and mild burns.[19]

Beverly Clark was among them. She had sustained bruises to her head when the trolley slammed into the open switch. During the scramble for the exits, one of her fingers had been broken. The finger was splinted, and Beverly went home with her family.[20]

Also released was Arleen Franzen, who had hung upside down from a window until Charles Kleim pulled her to safety. She was treated for bruises and burns to the bottoms of her feet.[21]

In spite of suffering what was described as a "broken left shoulder,"[22] 17-year-old Kyteria Cooper was not admitted to St. Bernard's. "They told me they couldn't admit me because I wasn't Catholic." She went home without treatment.[23]

But the most serious among the injured were the burn victims. Nearly every passenger not fortunate enough to exit the trolley immediately after the collision sustained some manner of burns to exposed body parts. Burns to the arms, hands, and faces were most common. Many women sustained burns to their legs and feet, which were exposed beneath their dresses and skirts. The last survivors to exit the trolley were the most seriously burned.

Povilas Abelkis, a Lithuanian refugee, had serious burns all over his body.[24] Fannie Powell, a clerk who was on her way home, sustained burns to her face, arms, and torso.[25] Catherine Johnson was en route to a christening in the far South Side community of Roseland where she was to serve as godmother to her niece, Rosemary. She had severe burns on her arms and torso. From her hospital bed, grateful at being spared, she murmured, "I thank thee, O blessed Virgin, I thank thee…"[26]

Perhaps the most critical was 60-year-old Mary Kortezynski, who lost her pink hat on the trolley. She was pushed out the rear window and landed hard on the pavement. Two other passengers landed on top of her. She, too, had severe burns to her arms, face, and torso. Still conscious, she asked authorities to take care when informing her husband of her condition, as he suffered from a heart ailment.[27]

Reverend R. L. Sidney might not have known that St. Bernard's was just a few blocks from 62nd Place and State Street. With passengers Vernon Anderson, Ben Head, and Alma Featherstone in his car, he drove quickly to the one hospital he did know—Provident, located at 426 E. 51st Street, nearly two miles away.

Anderson had suffered a broken nose in the scramble for the exits. He also had burns on his face. Compared with Head and Featherstone, he had been lucky. Caught at the rear of the car, Ben Head sustained first-, second-, and third-degree burns over his entire body. Alma Featherstone—her hair and clothing ablaze as she tumbled from the rear window—suffered similar injuries.[28]

With the absence of regional burn treatment facilities, Chicago hospitals treated their burn victims. At Provident Hospital, nurses carefully removed the burned remnants of clothing from Ben Head and Alma Featherstone. Both had received various degrees of burns, but the extent of third-degree burns to their bodies placed them in serious danger.

When skin is burned, capillaries begin to leak fluid, which builds up around the wound. In the case of large burns, fluid can begin to accumulate all over the body, not simply around the damaged tissue. Burns over 15 percent or more of the body can cause a victim to go into shock.

Head, Featherstone, and numerous other burn victims were given IVs to help replace these fluids. Urine output was closely monitored to make sure fluids were being adequately replaced.

Rendered essentially lifeless and with no pain receptors, skin in a third-degree burn is debrided or removed. In 1950, after the removal of dead tissue, the accepted practice was to cover burns in warm, moist dressing.

Skin is the body's first line of defense against bacterial infection. Without skin to protect them, burn victims are particularly susceptible to bacterial agents that could cause infection and threaten their lives. As the warm, moist environment of the dressings was a perfect breeding ground for bacteria, dressings had to be changed every one or two days.

As new tissue scabbed or formed beneath the dressing, a patient's pain from being repositioned and having dressings changed would have been excruciating. As a consequence, many patients were administered morphine.

In 1950, reporters and photographers were extended courtesies that through a twenty-first-century lens seem remarkable. Photographers who moments before had photographed the accident scene, stocked up on film and flashbulbs and raced to area hospitals on the heels of the ambulances. At St. Bernard's, Mary Pokorney was photographed lying on a gurney awaiting treatment, and then again after her entire head had been bandaged. She still held her raincoat, which she had brought to work that day. Her eyes—the only visible part of her face—looked up imploringly at an unseen caregiver.[29]

Arleen Franzen was photographed receiving treatment on her head. Later, looking exhausted, she was photographed again as she displayed a bandaged right hand.[30]

At Englewood Hospital, L. E. Potts's head, forearms, and hands were completely wrapped. His wife was shown standing along his bedside, a look of quiet anguish on her face.[31]

Ora Mae Bryant looked directly at the camera while at least three medical staff swaddled her neck in bandages. She was treated for shock and second-degree burns to her neck, face, and head.[32]

Photographers from *The Chicago Defender* were allowed to photograph patients at St. Bernard's and Provident hospitals. Edward White, wearing a robe and pajamas, sat in a wheelchair and displayed his bandaged right leg. Robert Nalls was shown in his bed nursing an injured back and digging into a plate of hospital food.[33]

Other photographs were considerably starker in contrast. Fannie Powell, hair disheveled, sleepy-eyed from the pain medication, lay on her belly to accommodate the burns on her legs. Ben Head lay propped up in bed. A pillow on his lap held his bandaged hands. Bandages covered his entire body save for a small portion of his face.[34]

Worst of all was Alma Featherstone. *The Defender* printed two photos of her, one sleeping on her side, and the other on her back, arms slightly raised in the direction of the camera. All visible parts of her body were bandaged except for the fingers on her left hand and a thin slit for her mouth and eyes.[35]

Most patients were fortunate enough to be released that evening or within 24 hours. Others, like Kortczynski, Featherstone, Abelkis, and Head, were going to have much longer roads to recovery.

Chapter
FIVE

Within an hour of the collision, the crowd around the crash site had swelled to a size to which the residents near 63rd and State were unaccustomed. Black smoke from the building fires drew neighbors and curiosity seekers like a beacon. Before long, the grassy area within the turnaround loop and the vacant lot adjacent to the Skonicki home were completely filled with onlookers. They lined the railroad embankment and the bridge over the flooded viaduct. Some climbed empty boxcars and railroad buildings to gain a better view as firefighters fought to contain the blaze. By 8:00 p.m., newspaper reporters estimated the crowd in excess of 15,000.[1]

At 7:27 p.m., Police Chief Raymond Crane, realizing he had far too few officers to manage the crowd, ordered all available officers from 28 districts to the scene.[2] A rallying center and temporary command post was set up at 61st and State, a little more than a block north of the turnaround. Officers who arrived assisted in detouring all non-emergency vehicles away from the crash site. Others formed a perimeter along the sidewalks on both sides of State, freeing the immediate area for firefighters and their equipment.

By now, more than 200 firefighters were fighting the blaze. Sixteen engine companies were present, as well as five hook-and-ladders and four rescue squads. Firefighting was being directed by Fire Chief Michael J. Corrigan, Chief Fire Marshal Anthony J. Mullaney, three deputy chiefs, a division marshal, and four battalion chiefs.[3]

In all, about 150 police officers responded to Crane's all-available call. In addition to Crane, officers were directed by Police Commissioner John C. Prendergast.

Police invoked Emergency Plan 5, a disaster plan created in 1948 as a means for coping with the most devastating of disasters, including an atomic blast.[4]

With the only working telephone on the block, the Skonicki home became a sort of media command center.[5] Reporters argued and fought over the phone, and then shouted their dispatches into the receiver over the din in the tiny kitchen and the living room. Walter Skonicki was interviewed by reporters from just about every major Chicago paper.

"I was lying on my couch in my living room. First there was a loud BOOM! Then there was a WHOOSH! I looked out the window and saw a big bunch of flames shooting two, three stories high. The flames were jumping around like big balls.

"People were running away from the trolley, screaming. Some were on fire. Fire was shooting out in all directions. The flames were so high I couldn't see either the streetcar or the truck part of the time.

"I ran outside. People in the trolley were smashing the windows trying to fight their way out. I saw their hands clawing at the guard bars on the windows. My daughter's car was parked in front of the house. I thought of moving it, but the heat was too intense. It burned up."[6]

Early radio reports estimated dozens of fatalities, both on board the trolley and in the buildings along State. As the accident interrupted all trolley service on State Street, families listened intently to these reports, hoping for some information about a loved one who was not yet home. The 36 Broadway/State shuttled several thousand passengers north and south every weekday evening.

Among the crowd at the scene were friends and family members of the missing who could not bear to stay home and wait for news reports or a telephone call from authorities. They, too, flocked to the scene, straining at the police line, describing a family member to anyone who would listen.

"Have you seen a tall, pretty girl with long black hair?"

"A short man in a brown jacket, white shirt, and porkpie hat?"

Neither police nor firefighters could help them.

Cook County Coroner A. L. Brodie arrived at the scene and, seeing the conditions of the remains, immediately ordered 33 squadrols—one for each of the victims—to bear them to the Cook County morgue.[7]

At about 8:45 p.m., the first squadrols backed their way down State Street and pulled alongside the curb. In short order, squadrols lined both sides of State Street near the turnaround like a macabre cab stand. White-coated morgue attendants were aided by police, firefighters, and civilians. Using collapsible canvas stretchers, they bore the remains away from the tarpaulin to one of a pair of waiting squadrols, their rear double doors open, an attendant waiting on the inside to haul in the stretcher and secure it for the ride to the morgue.

Among the bystanders pressed into service was 25-year-old Ed McElroy, a radio sports reporter who had learned of the accident on the radio and drove to the scene. As a member of the Army Air Corps during WWII, McElroy had once pulled a badly burned pilot from the wreckage of his plane.[8]

"The rescue workers had their hands full searching in the debris in the streetcar, so I pitched in when the bodies on the sidewalk had to be carried to the ambulances and squadrols nearby. Most of the bodies (were) burned beyond recognition and many were dismembered and torn apart.

"I didn't get sick. I don't know why. My senses of sight (touch), and smell were probably dulled and I could only think about getting the job over with."[9]

Among the onlookers along the perimeter surrounding the scene was Chicago Mayor Martin Kennelly, who pronounced it "…a sad, sad day for all Chicagoans."[10]

About 20 of Chief Crane's police officers lined the perimeter, intent on giving the men sufficient room to finish their job. The crowd, still quite large, was mostly behaved. Those closest to the tarpaulin stood nearly as stoic and somber as the police and firefighters themselves. Now and then a frantic voice called out and a man or woman strained at the line in search of a loved one.

Police Lt. William Hennessey—a 28-year veteran—did his best to calm them. "Take it easy, take it easy. Now's no time to look. We'll be taking the people to the county morgue soon."[11]

Arriving at hospitals only a few minutes after the victims, personal injury attorneys and their agents began to besiege survivors and their families, sometimes even before they had received medical treatment. Unlawful solicitation of legal business was grounds for disbarment, but even this threat did not deter them. Although a cause of the accident had not yet been established, an alarming number of "ambulance chasers" saw a cash cow. Armed with cards and contracts to retain services, they took advantage of distracted hospital security desks and entered rooms hoping to get victims and family members to sign retainers.

Some harassed survivors as they lay in their hospital beds. Most promised big money and quick settlements.[12]

Some of the parasites were not attorneys, but agents known as "runners" who pitched the services of a particular attorney and tried to induce prospective clients to sign a retainer. Some merely slipped them an attorney's business card with their own names scrawled on the back so the attorneys they represented could reward them with a finder's fee later on.

Most hospitals did their best to remove all ambulance chasers once they were discovered. On at least one occasion, a hospital staff member did the opposite. A doctor on staff at St. Bernard's brought an attorney to see Mary Kortezynski. He asked her to retain the attorney in a suit against the CTA. To her credit, Kortezynski refused and identified the doctor to authorities.[13]

One attorney told hospital staff that he was the brother of Alma Featherstone in an attempt to gain admittance to her room. He got in, but Featherstone refused to see him.

Robert Nalls, being treated at St. Bernard's, told a similar story, perhaps about the same attorney.[14]

At least one runner was caught soliciting business for an attorney and lost his day job because of it. Charles Keller, who was employed as a juvenile welfare worker for the State of Illinois, moonlighted as a runner for a personal injury attorney. When his name became connected with several business cards displayed by victims and their families, Keller admitted to his superiors that he was working as a runner on the side. He was let go, losing a $242-a-month job as a result.[15]

As names of survivors and victims were released to the media, attorneys began beating on the doors of grief-stricken relatives.

As his daughter Beverly spent a fitful night in her bed, Norman Clark fended off the overtures of attorneys until after midnight and then again on Friday morning. Frustrated with the constant invasion of privacy, he signed a retainer just to stop the advances of other attorneys.[16]

Although both white and black victims and their families were pressed by the ambulance chasers, a disproportionate number of African-Americans were targeted.

Clarence Edward, the director of public relations at Princeton Park, said that he was contacted by several attorneys. Realizing that many of the victims were Princeton Park residents, they promised to make it worth his while if he introduced them to victims' families. Edwards declined the offer.

"They said there would be something in it for me, but I turned them down. I'm sorry now I didn't keep their cards."[17]

Passenger Jeanette Williams said that at least eight attorneys visited her at her home, and two others identifying themselves as attorneys had called her on the phone.

"The one who said he was attorney Robert Krasnow was the most persistent. He was at the house three times. We have the card. He wouldn't leave Friday night until I said my husband had another attorney. But we don't have any attorney."[18]

Krasnow's card ended up in the hands of numerous other families. When reporters tracked him down, he claimed to have been referred to Mrs. Williams by a client. He denied having visited her three times, and he said he only gave her his business card when she requested it. He also claimed no knowledge of so-called runners who had signed the backs of his business cards and distributed them among victims and their families.

"I have never heard of any of those men, and I don't know of no reason why they should give anyone my card."[19]

One family who did respond to Krasnow's solicitations was the family of Kyteria Cooper. Refused treatment at St. Bernard's, Kyteria returned home and found that attorneys, including Krasnow, had already begun to make a pitch. Kyteria was only 17 years old and unable to sign a retainer. Both of her parents were illiterate, and they did not fully understand the document they were asked to sign. They did, however, respond to Krasnow's promise of a quick settlement for the most money possible.

Krasnow sent Kyteria to a downtown doctor later that week. The doctor examined her and x-rayed her shoulder, but he did not treat her. Several weeks later, Kyteria's father received a personal check from Krasnow's office in the amount of $2,000.00. The Coopers never knew the actual amount of the settlement, less Krasnow's fee. For more than 60 years, Kyteria believed that she and her family had been swindled.[20]

Within the week following the accident, *The Chicago Daily News* and other newspapers began to report on the ambulance chasers. *The Daily News* went person-to-person to survivors and their families, collecting business cards left by attorneys and their runners. They printed them in a special article, which included quotes from officials from the Illinois Bar Association warning against unlawful solicitations. The paper also printed a special feature entitled "How to Hire a Lawyer" in case of injury in a motor vehicle accident.[21] The article reminded readers they had up to six months to file a statement with the city and/or CTA, and then up to another six months to bring action. In any other accidents not involving the city, they had up to two years to file suit. Although many survivors and family members settled for the quick money, others bided their time. They followed the advice of the newspapers and family members, and waited for the results of the forthcoming investigations.

The bodies of all 33 victims began to arrive at the Cook County Morgue after 9:00 p.m. The attendant on duty, Frank Rissky, immediately began to implement a system that had been used four years earlier in the aftermath of the LaSalle Hotel fire. Rissky logged each victim into a ledger, temporarily assigning a number to each decedent since their identities were as yet unknown. Ninety-seven entries had preceded them in the ledger. The first victim was assigned the number "98."[22]

Rissky was soon assisted by about 40 Chicago police officers and other morgue attendants under Deputy Chief of Detectives William Touhy. They helped keep meticulous, detailed notes of personal effects that arrived with each victim. Rissky wrote the descriptions:

"No. 98: unidentified Negro woman, about 21 years old, found with a Du Sable High School ring, Class of 1945, on her finger. Initials 'F. C. C.' on inside of ring";

"No. 99: unidentified, elderly white woman wearing sturdy, Oxford shoes."[23]

Bodies were taken to the morgue basement where police officers and attendants arranged them as best they could. Most were laid on moveable gurneys. When those were all used, a few bodies were placed on examination tables used by the coroners.

Space limitations made the arrangement somewhat haphazard. None of the bodies were moved into the hallways, as officials deemed it prudent to contain the stench to one location.

The first family members and friends did not arrive until several hours later. Most saved the morgue as their last stop after inquiries made at area hospitals proved unsuccessful.

One of the first to arrive was Ed Rudenga, brother of Carol Rudenga, the page girl who was on her way to 63rd Street to shop for a bridesmaid's dress. Like thousands of other households, the Rudenga family had listened all evening to news reports on the radio. Carol, who had promised to call home when she stopped for a bite to eat, was long overdue. She was only 19, but she was a responsible girl who knew her family would worry about her. If she had been delayed, she certainly would have called.

That particular point bothered the family the most. Sensing the worst, Rudenga bypassed the hospitals, driving to the morgue instead where he found his sister beneath one of the shroud-covered tables in the basement.[24]

Selena Harris went to the morgue in search of her mother, Mrs. Ollie Smith, 58. At one point, while she passed through the narrow rows of tables in the morgue basement, she stopped and exclaimed, "Those are my mother's shoes! Oh, Lord God, help us."[25]

Not long after she was escorted from the room, a coroner's physician made a cursory examination of the body, determining that it belonged to a white woman. Ollie Smith was African-American. Believing she had just identified her mother's body, a numb Selena Harris was summoned from the hallway where she was asked to view the effects again. This time, she was able to identify the body of another woman, Number 116, as that of her mother.[26]

In some cases, loved ones sought at the morgue turned up safe and sound. The accident disrupted trolley service along the heavily trafficked 36-Broadway/State route for the remainder of the evening, leaving hundreds of commuters in exile searching for an alternate route home.

Those forced to disembark near the accident scene may have joined the crowd and watched for several hours as the drama continued to unfold. As they stared disbelievingly, they may not have thought to contact relatives, who by now had listened to the news on the radio and were beginning to fear the worst. Employers began to call the morgue in search of workers who had not shown up for the evening shift.

A sizable number of Chicagoans did not yet have telephones in their homes. Some stranded travelers had no way of contacting loved ones. The fears of many families were assuaged only when the missing showed up on the front doorstep many hours later.

On at least one occasion, an inquiry made at the morgue ended happily. Edward T. McFadden had gone to the morgue in search of his brother Martin. He brought with him Dr. G. R. McLaughlin, a dentist, who was Martin's brother-in-law. "Martin had taken that streetcar for years, and he always telephones when he's going to be late," McLaughlin said. Just before the pair headed downstairs to the basement, a telephone call came in. The missing brother was safe at home. Apparently, Martin had gone out on a social engagement after work and not arrived home until after 2:00 a.m.[27]

As they logged personal items, morgue attendants were able to make tentative identifications based on effects that contained names and addresses. Wallets, purses, and pockets that survived the fire were found to contain the charred remnants of driver's licenses, bills, letters, and other items.

Chief Deputy Coroner Jack Pryzbylinski found a wallet on the remains of one body, which contained several cards bearing the name of Martha Jankauskis. Przybylinski telephoned the Jankauskis home. Her three brothers were able to make an identification later that evening.[28]

Mrs. Hazel O'Neal was able to identify her mother, Mrs. Alean Fisher, 48, by a bill found in her purse.[29]

Mr. and Mrs. Chris Vos identified the body of their daughter, Arvis, 20, by her wristwatch.[30]

Edward Everett Werner, 65, who was probably the old man to whom Beverly Clark had given her seat, was identified by the landlord of his building by a key found on his body.[31]

Floreine Foster's mother identified her by her Du Sable High School ring. The initials "F. C. C." were from her maiden name, when she had been Floreine Cater.[32]

It was close to midnight when Nell Medley and her husband, Ray, arrived at the morgue. They had left her sister Mamie Manning at the duplex they shared on Berwyn Avenue. Earlier that evening, radio reports had confirmed that motorman Paul Manning was among the dead in the trolley. To that point, neither police nor the CTA had placed a call to the family.

Grief-stricken, Mamie Manning could not bring herself to accompany her sister and brother-in-law. She remained at home and sat for the Medley's four-year-old son.

The Medleys gave a physical description of Paul Manning to morgue attendants, as well as a description of any personal effects that he might have carried with him. They took a seat on a wooden bench in the hallway and waited to be called.

Like her sister, Nell Medley was an attractive woman. As she sat next to her husband, occasionally dabbing her eyes with a handkerchief, photographers snapped her picture.

When the time came, Nell accompanied her husband as far as the basement door, where the horrific smell made her head swim and drove her away. Ray Medley shouldered the burden alone. He went downstairs, escorted by police sergeant James Mulqueen, who led him to one of the 33 gurneys in the room.

At the foot of one of the gurneys, Mulqueen produced two items—a plain gold wedding band, and a railroad pocket watch. Medley confirmed that both items had belonged to his brother-in-law. Manning's body had shielded the watch, which had stopped at 6:33 p.m. and was used by police to establish the time of the accident.

Mulqueen allowed Medley to view the remains, which were covered with a sheet. Paul Manning had been a big man, but the shrouded figure suggested otherwise. Pinned at the front of the car where the fire had been most intense, Manning crumpled to the floor and curled into the fetal position. His body had been completely desiccated. Medley later told his wife that the body on the gurney was dramatically reduced in size—no bigger than that of a child and weighing perhaps 60 pounds.[33]

More than 200 people entered the basement in search of loved ones through the early morning hours of Friday, May 26, and continuing into Memorial Day weekend. Dental records were sought to aid in the identification of the most severely damaged bodies. In one case, two different families claimed the same body as that of a loved one. Positive identification was made all the more difficult as both of the missing individuals had almost identical bridgework.[34]

Coroner A. L. Brodie hastily assembled a Coroner's Inquest jury that released bodies already identified by family members to local funeral parlors. By Tuesday morning after the holiday, only a handful of remains had not yet been claimed.

Chapter
SIX

When the trolleys and "L" consolidated to form the CTA in 1947, the new Transit Authority was governed by a seven-member board. Four of the seven members, including the board chairman, were appointed by the mayor of Chicago, thus giving the mayor's office considerable power over the company. Mayor Edward Kelly appointed four members in 1945, including the CTA's first chairman, Philip Harrington.[1] When Harrington died while recuperating from surgery in February 1949, Mayor Martin J. Kennelly took his time appointing Harrington's successor. It proved a judicious move on the part of Kennelly, as the best candidate for the job was not yet available.

Ralph Budd was a midwestern railroad man who turned 70 in 1949. He had worked for railroads since 1899 when he got his first job as a draftsman for the Chicago Great Western Railroad. He proved to be a talented engineer, and during the first decade of the twentieth century, he was hired by a former employer to design and build the Trans-Isthmian Railway through the dense jungles of Panama at the same time the canal was being dug there. Against impossible odds and unfriendly terrain, he met every deadline and finished the project ahead of schedule.[2]

At 33, he was appointed chief engineer of the Great Northern Railroad, becoming its president at age 40 in 1919. He was a capable administrator, known for eliminating waste and improving the comfort, speed, and reliability of the passenger railways over which he presided. In 1932, he took over the Chicago, Burlington & Quincy Railroad—"the Burlington," as it was known. During the lean years of the Great Depression when other railroads sank into receivership, Budd managed to increase ridership and make improvements to passenger travel that lasted for decades.[3]

Together, he and auto designer Edward Budd (a distant relation) created the streamlined "Burlington Zephyr" in 1934, which ran from Denver to Chicago from "dusk-to-dawn."

In accordance with age restrictions that he had imposed years earlier, he retired from the Burlington in August 1949. He turned down an offer of a lectureship at Northwestern University, modestly arguing that he had little of import to offer academia.[4]

Budd was a meticulous man. He loved history, particularly railroad history. He belonged to numerous historical societies and contributed to many others. Though a businessman all his adult life, he resembled a courtly gentleman-farmer. He was tall and thick-bodied, mostly bald on top, with hound dog eyes behind thick wire spectacles. He had a warm sense of humor and good people skills. Upon leaving his office, visitors had the sense that Budd took a personal as well as a professional interest in them.[5]

On September 1, Mayor Kennelly introduced Budd as the CTA's second chairman. At his first press conference, Budd conceded that he could not lower fares, but he promised to do all he could to make the CTA more reliable for its riders.

"I like to spend money," he told the press on his first day, "but I like to make it first. I'll spend money as fast as we can make it. Our best chance for success is to get the CTA on a business basis that everyone will recognize as good business."[6]

Among his early moves was the procurement of an $11 million loan from a consortium of Chicago banks for the purchase of motor buses and improvements to the elevated lines.[7]

In an effort to learn about his vehicles, he became a daily rider of public transportation, often conversing with motormen and conductors to learn the ins and outs of their trade. In Budd, the CTA had perhaps the best possible man to lead them through a critical period.[8]

When the streetcar crash occurred, Budd had been in office less than nine months. Accidents involving CTA vehicles were not unusual, but as details of the event trickled in, it was clear that this one would require very special care. Although no reports place Budd at the accident scene on May 25, he and his staff did much in its aftermath.

Budd knew that the next several weeks were likely to be trying ones for the company. On the morning of May 26, information as to the cause of the accident was still sketchy. With Manning dead, there was no first-person account from the driver of the principal vehicle. Still, eyewitness accounts seemed to agree that Budd's motorman had been at fault.

The morning papers contained interviews of motorists who had been traveling behind Manning's streetcar just before the collision. Calvin Dahl, a building contractor who was in the vicinity after having picked up his dog at a nearby kennel, had just made a right-hand turn into the southbound lanes of State Street when he was passed by Manning's trolley.

"I was right behind the streetcar when I got on State. It was going so fast, it didn't stop at (Sixty-first) and up ahead at what looked like a switch, there was a supervisor waving to it to slow down. I slowed down but the streetcar didn't. It hit that switch and it swerved. It smashed that truck right in the middle and the truck went up about five feet."[9]

Based on the speed of his own vehicle, Dahl told reporters he thought the streetcar was traveling at about 30 mph.

Robert Mitchell, a building contractor traveling with three co-workers, said they had trailed Manning's trolley since 59th Street. They, too, thought the car was traveling at about 30 mph, and noted that a man in a CTA uniform had tried to flag the trolley down just before it entered the switch.[10]

Budd allowed the experts to sift through the data of the crash, keeping mum in the press about the accident's causes. Lawsuits were most assuredly going to follow, but the CTA's insurance would take care of that.

What worried Budd much more was the forthcoming damage to the company's reputation. As he had done with other companies under his watch, Budd was rebuilding and redefining the CTA's integrity in the eyes of the public. Now he had to explain why more than 30 CTA passengers were dead, and as many as 50 more were injured.

To his credit, Budd never tried to minimize the company's culpability, but he did his best to control the damage already done. He took the initiative almost immediately.

Budd met with CTA general manager Walter J. McCarter and attorney James O. Dwight. While Coroner A. L. Brodie organized his own Coroner's Inquest, the CTA agreed to hold an inquest of its own at the CTA offices on May 26, less than 24 hours after the accident. Principal witnesses included flagger Charles Kleim, motorman George Hartwig, supervisor Peter Duggan, and conductor William Liddell. All were expected to tell their stories before the press.[11]

Budd presided over the meeting and was joined by McCarter, Dwight, and CTA traffic engineer Stanley Forsythe. "There isn't a thing in the world the CTA wants to hide," Budd assured the officials and reporters in attendance, "but we want the facts to come out and (with) no distortion of facts."[12]

With that, Budd revealed that motorman Paul Manning had been involved in ten accidents spread over the course of the past year and a half. Budd was quick to point out the fact that only two of the accidents were considered "chargeable" to Manning, however. Both of these occurred while Manning was driving buses, and both caused only minor damage to property resulting in modest settlements.[13]

Prompted by reporters, he added that he considered this to be a "good" record. The revelation created a murmur through the crowded chamber, prompting attorney James Dwight to say, "The poor guy is dead. Let's not make it too hard on him."[14]

Budd also said that he expected claims against the CTA to be numerous. Although the elevated lines were insured by Lloyd's of London, at the time, the CTA bus and trolley lines were self-insured. A fund containing $5 million was always set aside for liability and property damage. That amount was maintained by using 4½ percent of trolley revenue each month, which translated to about $450,000 monthly.[15]

Budd and his staff also discussed streetcar safety features, which were being called into question. CTA traffic engineer Stanley Forsythe explained that although doors could only be opened by the conductor or the motorman, the CTA was comfortable with what he called a "calculated risk." The alternative—namely, giving passengers free access to the doors of a trolley at all times—could just as easily imperil passengers.[16]

Forsythe went on to say that only the center exit—the one through which Beverly Clark and several others had escaped—was equipped with an emergency handle. Budd commented that even if the rear doors had been equipped with emergency handles, it would have been to no avail. In his opinion, the rapid spread of flames would still have claimed many victims.[17]

Later, Budd took a swipe at gasoline haulage in the city. He referred to gas trucks that traveled busy thoroughfares as a "constant menace" and cited several large U. S. cities that had ordinances in place restricting their operation. He urged the City Council to discuss the implementation of a suitable plan for Chicago.[18]

After finishing opening remarks, Budd called on those CTA employees who had been at the scene to give their accounts of the accident. The first to tell his story was Charles Kleim.

Kleim looked relaxed in spite of a fitful night's rest. After giving a statement to CTA officials at the scene of the accident, he returned home very late. His children besieged him with questions, but backed off when an exhausted Kleim could only offer a few, tired words.

The following morning, Kleim wore a two-toned sport coat with a short, wide tie. He smiled when he posed for a photo with Ralph Budd, looking directly at his boss as the shutter snapped. On the stand, he gave a concise account of his actions as Manning's trolley came into view.[19]

Kleim explained that he saw the trolley approaching from the north when it was about two blocks away. He began signaling when it was a block away, adding that he even put one foot on the switch handle to make himself more conspicuous to the motorman.

"But he kept right on coming." Kleim demonstrated the palms-down motion he used, imploring Manning to ease up. He continued to signal, becoming more agitated as Manning neared. Fearing for his own safety, he jumped out of the trolley's path just before it entered the switch.[20]

"All of a sudden I could hear it—BANG! There was a flash of flame and black smoke."[21]

Kleim described how he lowered the trolley pole and then helped "six or eight passengers"[22] escape through a rear window until the flames drove him away.

When asked how fast he thought the car had been traveling as it approached the switch, Kleim gave an estimate of 30 miles an hour.[23]

At that point, Budd interjected, commenting that he thought Kleim's 30-mph estimate was an exaggeration. Mustering the authority of a man with 50 years of experience in rail transportation, he explained that the trolley would most likely have derailed immediately had it entered the switch at such a high rate of speed. He suggested a speed of 20 miles per hour. At any rate, he thought it likely that Manning had been traveling "a little too fast" to make the switch.[24]

Motorman George Hartwig said he had seen the crash, but he was unable to estimate the trolley's speed prior to impact. He also described Paul Manning's final moments as the motorman, pinned within the wreckage, struggled within the flames.[25]

When William Liddell took the stand, he still had not been home. Someone had retrieved a black Sunday suit from his house, and he wore it on the stand. He spoke just above a whisper, stopping several times to compose himself. He appeared nervous and dazed, still suffering the aftereffects of the accident, which had happened less than 24 hours earlier.[26]

He began by describing the scene inside the trolley immediately after the impact:

"The only thing I know is that all of a sudden I was on the floor. There were flames all over the car. People were rushing for the exit. I set the mechanism for the rear doors so they would open. The next thing I know they were pouring like a wave out the rear windows and they pushed me out with them."[27]

Bruised and traumatized, Liddell said he accepted a ride from a passing motorist who took him to a local doctor. Liddell could not remember the doctor's name. After leaving the doctor's office, he told officials that he went to a friend's house where he ended up spending the night. He refused to disclose the name of the friend.[28]

Listening within the chambers, Traffic Police Chief Michael Ahern was not impressed with Liddell's testimony. At the conclusion of the hearing, when Kleim, Hartwig, Peter Duggan, and Liddell were taken to police headquarters to give official statements, Ahern had Liddell placed under arrest for leaving the scene of the accident. Liddell was ordered to appear in traffic court later that summer. The CTA posted his $100 bond.[29]

As CTA officials discussed Paul Manning's actions, Mamie Manning did her best to defend her husband and answer some of the charges against him.

"They're trying to put it all on Paul," she told reporters. "They're trying to lay this accident (on) him."[30]

Reporters asked Mrs. Manning about the allegations that her husband's trolley was traveling at 30 miles per hour when it entered the switch. Her answer touched on a familiar theme.

"He had to make his time. He always had to make his time. Well, now he has made it. They take off runs, and then they drive the men to make them keep their schedules. He was always harping on that. If they make their time, don't think they're not speeding."[31]

Ray Medley, Manning's brother-in-law, took a more practical position:

"Why would he be going 30 mph—even if he were going straight ahead—on a downhill grade ahead of him so near to Sixty-third Street, a dangerous intersection?"[32]

Medley was referring to the fact that Manning was less than 100 yards from his stop at the safety island just north of the intersection of 63rd and State streets. Near that point, State Street began its downward slope toward the viaduct.

"He would have slid right across. He had to stop at Sixty-third."[33]

For the first time, Medley suggested that Manning might not have been at fault.

"I heard talk down at the barn that he was supposed to be the first car to go through—that the water under the viaduct had receded enough. Did the flagman really wave him down—or wave him to go ahead?"[34]

Other motormen defended Manning when they complained that their schedules together with dense loads of passengers often made it necessary for them to speed. In the *Chicago Sun-Times*, on May 28, several motormen, conductors, and other CTA officials argued over the expectations regarding schedules.

One motorman, an eight-year veteran, said he and others "...take chances we wouldn't take otherwise to keep a schedule. Anybody would have accidents at the speeds we have to go."[35]

A conductor quoted in the same article said he sometimes feared for his own safety as motormen along his route did their best to make a 7½-mile route in 43 minutes.

"Any sane person would know that the speed of the cars should be cut."[36]

Any act of God or minor traffic inconvenience—bad weather, a long stop light, or a particularly busy corner with many boarding passengers—could knock a motorman off schedule.

"Then we have to start taking chances. They keep after us to make the schedule."[37]

CTA dispatchers, supervisors, and other officials interviewed for the piece took issue with the notion that schedules were expected to be kept at all costs. One official said that safety never took a backseat to schedules. He also disagreed with the motormen's idea that they had to put on excessive speed to make schedules.

A dispatcher said he knew of no CTA directive compelling motormen to exceed the speed limit to stay on schedule. But he also said that with the new, smooth-riding Green Hornets, motormen might not even realize they were speeding.

The question of trolley speed would play a pivotal part in the Coroner's Inquest, which was scheduled to open on Thursday, June 1, after the Memorial Day holiday.

Monday, May 29, was the 82nd annual observance of Memorial Day and only the fifth time the holiday had been observed since the end of World War II. Chicagoans visited churches and cemeteries, remembering absent brothers and sons, husbands and fathers whose faces were yet so easily recalled. Those who visited gravesides that day might have seen the first few families burying victims of the trolley crash. At least seven of the 33 were buried on Memorial Day, including John Storey, Lewis Howlett, Frances Mennite, Katie Westerveld, Theresa Axteld, Mel Wilson, and Carol Rudenga.

Earl Sue Sharpe, the seamstress who died returning home from Du Sable High School, was buried on June 2. Du Sable's "Hi Jinx" show went off without a hitch and received excellent reviews in *The Defender*. Earl Sue was acknowledged for her work as a costume designer for the show.[38]

The family of Luella Phillips, a schoolteacher who died on the trolley, assumed her body had been too badly burned to allow for an open casket at her memorial service. Embalmers at the O. F. Douglas Funeral Parlor at 4521 S. State employed a relatively new process of "derma surgery." Using photos provided by the family, they were able to restore Luella's face to a reasonable, recognizable likeness.[39]

On Friday, June 2, *The Defender* co-sponsored a "Sympathy" meeting with residents of Princeton Park and the nearby Lillydale community for victims of the accident. The meeting was held at the St. James Methodist Church, 9258 S. Lafayette, in Lillydale. Clarence Edward, the Princeton Park public relations director, was one of the speakers. Several ministers from local churches also spoke.

The Defender urged residents to attend and "lend support to the movement for safer transportation and better service for far Southsiders."[40]

William Liddell returned home to find a letter addressed to him from a woman named Ceola Glen. In the letter—written in a rambling, slightly cryptic style—Glen thanked Liddell for saving her in the confusion after the collision. Liddell passed the letter on to his superiors at the CTA, who immediately saw a public relations opportunity. The letter was promptly released to the press. Several Chicago papers ran portions of the letter. *The Chicago Defender* printed it in its entirety:

> Mr. William Liddell—
>   I want to thank you for helping me up from the floor. I don't remember how I got out of that fire. I have six children and cannot pay you. If I could,

I would give you millions of dollars. I shall never forget this. I was sort of prejudiced but now I am not.

I remember only two things in that car. (One) You telling people "to stand back from the door" (Two) "To step this way, here's an open window." After that I don't remember anything. I forgot what the people looked like. I forgot what everyone on the car was like. I remember men helping me from the ground. How I got on the ground I don't know.

I ran, ran, and ran until I fell down. Everyone was going to the fire. It seems as if it was right behind me. I didn't get a scar on me not even a scratch. I forgot how to spell, to see.

I don't even want to talk about it to anyone. If you hadn't pulled me from the floor I would have been dead. It seems like thousands of people were on that car the way they were ganged up to the door.

My friend took me to the country because I am so nervous. I still don't know how I got out. Only one thing happened to me. I can't tell you about that, it is for ladies only. Also I can't remember for the life of me, the face of those poor people. Matter-of-fact, I can't remember your face, either.

I was going to 71st St. to get some pansies for my back yard and to find a cock-key to turn water on the outside of the building. I am sorry I don't have any way to show my appreciation for your helping me. You saved my life.

I haven't told my mother and father about this. My dad is sick, he probably would worry about it. I told my kids I got off two blocks away so that they couldn't tell my mother how I almost died.

Thank you again and again, you did your best. I know because I was there. Thanks again, again and a million times. Funny I don't know how or why I got out. Was it you that pushed me through a window? Everytime I try to remember I get a headache. Thanks again—

"/s/" Mrs. Ceola Glen[41]

Ceola Glen was something of an enigma. By her own account, her injuries were not serious enough to warrant medical treatment, explaining why her name did not appear on any hospital injury report. She was never interviewed by police or press. Her appearance led authorities to wonder if any other survivors had failed to "check in" after the fact. The Red Cross urged any other survivors to contact their Wabash Avenue offices.

William Liddell had trouble remembering Ceola Glen, too. He could not picture her, nor could he remember helping a specific woman from the floor amid the chaos within the car. But he confided to his family that he appreciated her letter, and he kept it in a safe place for the rest of his life.[42]

Summer storms continued to pass through the city, leaving flooded underpasses and a concerned populace in their wake. One Friday, June 2, just eight days after the accident, a severe storm flooded 20 underpasses throughout the city, including the viaduct at 63rd and State.

Trolley traffic along State Street was short-turned once again at the 62nd Place turnaround. Not taking any chances, the CTA placed five men at the turnaround instead of the requisite one or two. As an added precaution, a police squad car stood parked nearby.[43]

Streetcar accidents, which usually escaped the newspapers or were buried deep within their pages, now made headlines. Three days after the accident, two Green Hornets collided on Western Avenue near Belmont. A few Lane Tech High School students were shaken up, but the story became front page news when it was revealed that a large gas truck was trailing one of the trolleys and missed colliding with the vehicle by several feet.[44]

Besides a respectful sympathy for the victims and their families, public response to the accident played out in the papers in letters to the editor and op-ed pieces. The accident made Chicagoans sensitive—and in some cases, hypersensitive—to safety issues on their daily commutes and around their own neighborhoods.

In a special meeting held on Sunday, May 28, Ralph Budd and the CTA board passed a resolution expressing sympathy for the victims, survivors, and their families. It read as follows:

> Whereas, a tragic accident occurred on the evening of May 25, 1950, causing the deaths of thirty-three or more persons and the injury of others as the result of a collision between a streetcar and a gasoline truck on State St. near 63rd St. in Chicago; and
>
> Whereas, the tracks at the intersection and the equipment used were in good condition, and this appears to have been one of those unfortunate events difficult to avoid due to the intervention of fortuitous circumstances which occur in the operation of transportation; and
>
> Whereas, the Chicago Transit Board shares with the community a feeling of deep sadness and regret that this accident should have taken place and these citizens should have lost their lives or been injured;
>
> Now therefore be it resolved by the Chicago Transit Board of the Chicago Transit Authority:

1. That Chicago Transit Board hereby expresses to the families and friends of those who lost their lives its sincere sympathy in this tragic hour and also expresses to those who were injured the deepest regret of this Board;

2. That the Board expresses its gratitude to the members of the Police and Fire Departments of the City of Chicago, to the Red Cross, to individuals present and to employees of the Authority for the valiant assistance given to those injured;

3. That this resolution be spread upon the minutes of the Chicago Transit Board of the meeting of May 26, 1950.[45]

Budd had done what he could to control the damage done to the CTA's reputation over the seven days following the accident. He had stood unflinching before the press, answering their questions to the best of his abilities—never offering too much information, but never shirking the responsibilities that rested on his shoulders. At the CTA inquest, he had circumvented a public relations disaster, offering a brief but plausible account of the accident and a preliminary sketch of its causes. He had acted as a chairman should in such a case—with contrition, but also with authority and intelligence.

Budd also knew that he had merely laid a foundation for the events that were to follow. A Blue Ribbon jury was about to explore all mitigating factors associated with the accident. The Coroner's Inquest was set to open on June 1. Although Budd was not a native Chicagoan, he was no stranger to the inner workings of a political machine. In a Chicago courtroom, anything could happen and often did. The real drama was yet to come.

Chapter
SEVEN

Cook County Coroner A. L. Brodie was a gruff machine politician who had served at his post for ten years. Brodie was a politician and not a medical doctor—not an uncommon occurrence in big cities at the time. He was born in Chicago in 1889, hawked newspapers on State Street as a boy, joined the Illinois National Guard in his twenties, and served in World War I.

His political career began in the 1920s when he hustled votes in the 24th Ward on the city's West Side. He ascended the ladder quickly, receiving appointments to various patronage positions, including park district secretary and chief clerk in both the State Auditor's office and the Coroner's office. He also served as a hospital superintendent.[1]

In addition to his position as coroner, he served briefly as interim Cook County sheriff in 1943 following the death of the previous sheriff. What Brodie lacked in medical knowledge he made up for as a hands-on, no-nonsense administrator. He possessed an unsettling scowl made more ominous by his impressive jowls and a bulbous nose reddened from rosacea. By 1950, he had already suffered the first of a series of heart attacks that would end his life in August 1952.[2]

Brodie was no stranger to tragedy. In 1946, he oversaw the inquest into the fire at the downtown LaSalle Hotel on LaSalle and Madison, in which 61 people had died. Then as now, all eyes had been watching. Within 24 hours of the trolley crash, he assembled a panel of six inquest jurors to begin hearing evidence in the investigation of the accident. Brodie presided over the brief preliminary hearing, which convened on Friday, May 26 at the Cook County Building. After releasing bodies to funeral parlors, Brodie adjourned the inquest until June 1, telling reporters he would impanel a "Blue Ribbon" jury composed of appropriate experts capable of sifting through the mountains of evidence in the case. He also said he would subpoena "anyone and everyone" who could aid in the investigation.[3]

In all, Brodie impaneled 12 jurors—the maximum allowed for a Coroner's Inquest. He retained three of the original six jurors from the May 26 session, including the director of the Motor Transportation Bureau of the National Safety Council, Mr. Paul H. Coburn. Other jurors with backgrounds in traffic safety included Col. Franklin Kreml, director of the Traffic Institute at Northwestern University, and James S. Baker, research director at the same institute.

The rest of the jurors were a varied lot. Ludwig Friedlander was the vice president of Chippewa Paper Stock. Major Lyndon C. Wilson was a registered engineer. Lucius C. Harper was the executive director of *The Chicago Defender*. Also from *The Defender* was Dr. E. A. Woles, who served as company physician for the paper. A second physician, Dr. Troy M. Smith, also joined the jury. Thomas H. Mooney was the lone civilian or "nonexpert" juror.

The jury's foreman was Professor J. J. Ahern of the Illinois Institute of Technology, who was an expert on fire prevention and safety.[4]

Brodie reconvened the inquest at 11:00 a.m. on June 1. More than 200 people crowded the fifth-floor County Board room to hear the proceedings. Prominent among them was Mamie Manning, who had brought along an attorney hired by her family. The room bore a somber atmosphere made all the more so as Brodie began the proceedings by reading the names of those who had perished in the accident—a litany of the dead. As he read, veiled women clad in black broke down in audible sobs as they recognized the names of loved ones. Few left their seats in the crowded confines, intent upon learning why 33 people had lost their lives.[5]

Brodie commissioned the jury to establish the causes of the crash, and he enlisted the help of more than 20 witnesses, many of whom were at the scene of the accident and others whose expertise could shed light on the events. The day was to have three parts. After hearing witness testimony, jurors would be shuttled to the scene of the accident to view the switch and the wreck of the gas truck. From there they would travel to the car barn at 77th and Vincennes to inspect the remains of trolley No. 7078.

Attorneys present included R. F. Kelly, representing the CTA, and Leonard Bosgarf, hired by the family of Paul Manning. Police and fire officials included Fire Marshal Anthony J. Mullaney and Chief of Traffic Police Michael J. Ahern. CTA employees slated to testify included supervisor Peter Duggan, motorman George Hartwig, and motorman/ flagger Charles Kleim. Brodie was expected to call about a dozen other witnesses who would shed light on numerous circumstances surrounding the crash.

Early witnesses described the accident scene, including the condition of the switch, trolley cables, and vehicles. One of the first to testify was Mullaney, the city's venerable chief fire marshal. He was nearing 60—a thick-bodied, white-haired bulldog of a man who was first named to the position of fire marshal in 1933. Like Brodie, he had seen his share of calamitous fires. As testament, his office contained two lamp fixtures from the LaSalle Hotel—one, saucer-shaped and in pristine condition, and the other, melted like a child's deflated punch ball.[6]

Mullaney described finding the trolley switch in the open position, and pointed out that the switch had been plugged to keep it open. The overhead cables melted in the fire and hung at irregular intervals like jungle vines. Mullaney suggested that a spark from the fallen cable or from the gas truck's muffler had ignited the gasoline. The trolley pole had been lowered. The rear wheels were off the track, the derailment occurring either as the car entered the switch or as a result of the impact with the gas truck.[7]

Mullaney continued, detailing the remains of the streetcar after the fire was struck—a battered, ruined hulk, almost completely gutted of any recognizable objects. Those windows not shattered in the collision were broken by passengers seeking some means of escape. Others cracked in the extreme heat of the fire. Inside the car, all the seats had burned completely away, leaving only their metal frames behind. The flames had eaten away much of the floor, which had partially collapsed as the vehicle was towed away. The rear doors were closed and had to be pried open by firefighters. Mullaney also described the gruesome discovery of charred bodies stacked like cordwood against these doors.[8]

As Mullaney spoke, photographs were distributed among the jurors, which detailed the accident scene and the condition of the trolley. At least one photo showed the remains of passengers clustered around the rear door.

The Inquest was interrupted momentarily when Robert Mitchell, a 19-year-old eyewitness scheduled to testify, apparently fainted after viewing some of the photographs over the shoulder of a juror who was seated in front of him. Mitchell was carried from the chambers by other members of the gallery.[9]

Jurors were also moved by the photos, and they began to question Mullaney:

Juror: "Have you an opinion whether the tremendous pressure of bodies against the door caused failure to open them?"

Mullaney: "I think the impact and surge of the car as it swung hurled people against the doors."[10]

Many survivors recalled being thrown from their seats as the car lurched suddenly as it entered the switch. But jurors had difficulty believing that this was the primary cause of the pile-up at the rear doors.

> JUROR: "You don't think the people piled against the doors made their way there in an attempt to escape?"
>
> MULLANEY: "Some, yes. But I believe others were flung from their seats at the crash."[11]

Jurors also pressed Mullaney for information on events just prior to the collision.

> JUROR: "When was the motorman of the death car notified of the hazard caused by the flooded underpass?"
>
> MULLANEY: "My inquiry showed he was notified only at the scene by the CTA flagman, Charles G. Kleim."[12]
>
> JUROR: "What is the practice on approaching such a switch?"
>
> MULLANEY: "My understanding is that practice is to reduce speed to five miles an hour."[13]

R. F. Kelly, attorney for the CTA, interjected here.

> KELLY: "There is no flat minimum; speed should be reduced sufficiently so the motorman can have visible evidence whether the switch is open or closed."[14]

Brodie excused Mullaney, although the fire marshal would accompany jurors on their investigations of both vehicles later in the day. Evidence uncovered at the crash site and at the car barn at 77th and Vincennes would call Mullaney's testimony into question once again.

Next to take the stand was Capt. Michael J. Ahern, Chief of Chicago's Traffic Bureau. Armed with a report prepared by one of his lieutenants, Ahern talked about the movements of both vehicles. The gas truck was owned by the Sprout & Davis Co. out of Whiting, Indiana. The driver,

Mel Wilson, was described by the company president as "one of our best, with a perfect safety record."[15] Wilson had not yet made a delivery that day. He passed through the underpass and was climbing the grade up State Street toward the turnaround when his truck was struck by Manning's trolley. Upon investigation, the truck was found to be in second gear in which, according to Ahern's report, it could not travel more than eight miles an hour.

Ahern offered a theory as to Manning's actions. Assuming that the motorman had not been informed of the hazard by other supervisors along his route, Manning saw northbound traffic emerging from the underpass and simply assumed he would continue through the underpass without impediment. The theory did not explain, however, why Manning had not seen Charles Kleim.[16]

Ahern described Manning's route. He had departed the Clark-Devon car barn at 5:05 p.m. and shuttled passengers along Devon Avenue, Broadway Avenue, and Clark, Division, and State streets. A supervisor noted that Manning had arrived at the corner of State and Van Buren streets at 5:57 p.m. To that point, Manning had traveled a distance of 9.7 miles in 52 minutes.[17]

Manning was due to arrive at 63rd and State at 6:34 p.m. The collision occurred at 6:33 p.m. Ahern said that the exact time was ascertained by a watch recovered from the wrecked trolley. Ahern didn't know it at the time, but the watch had belonged to the motorman.

At the time of the collision, Manning had traveled 16.5 miles in 88 minutes. Ahern explained that this would have accounted for an average speed of about 20 miles per hour. But this estimate did not include the numerous occasions along the route when the vehicle was at a complete stop. *The Chicago Herald-American*, in its evening edition on June 1, quoted "a public transportation expert" who explained that when one factored in the time needed to take on and discharge passengers, Manning's average speed was much faster. In fact, he would have had to move at speeds up to 40 miles an hour in order to cover the 16.5 miles in the allotted time.[18]

Based on his experience with the new Green Hornets, Ahern probably would have agreed with the estimate. Trolley speed had been an issue of some importance to him even before the accident. Jury foreman Prof. J. J. Ahern (no relation) asked the chief what the posted speed limit was at State Street near the site of the accident. "Twenty-five miles an hour," was Capt. Ahern's reply.[19] But what he said next took both the jury and gallery by surprise.

Ahern explained that neither the City of Chicago nor the State of Illinois had ever imposed speed limits on streetcars. Indeed, prior to 1936 when the PCCs first came online, and later in 1947 with the introduction of the Green Hornets, such a speed restriction had not been necessary. Still, after more than a decade of service on Chicago streets and after numerous accidents in which trolley speed was a contributing factor, no speed restrictions had been imposed on trolley cars or buses. "Even if the motorman had been traveling 50 miles an hour," Ahern commented, "we couldn't ticket him."[20]

Ahern sensed that the crowd in the County Board Room that day had no idea just how fast the Green Hornets could travel. He continued, telling the jury that he knew for a fact that the new cars could travel at a speed of 55 miles an hour. He based his figure on a personal experience.

One day, as he drove into work down Broadway Avenue, Ahern's automobile was passed by a Green Hornet that was obviously exceeding the posted speed limit. Ahern accelerated and pulled alongside the car. When he glanced at his own speedometer, he was amazed that both he and the trolley were zooming along at 55 miles per hour! Ahern couldn't believe his eyes.

Prohibited by law to stop the trolley and cite the motorman, Ahern reduced his own speed and watched the trolley go. But he marked the moment, and he waited for an opportunity to do something about what he considered to be this latest threat to traffic safety on his watch.[21]

"A streetcar or trolley bus can be driven as fast as its power permits— without police interference—under present law, " Ahern stated. "Only an amendment to the state traffic law could change this."[22]

The following day, the CTA felt it necessary to issue a response to Ahern's claim and to reassure its riders that their vehicles were not capable of such speeds. A CTA spokesman was quoted in *The Daily News*:

"We have no desire for a quarrel with Chief Ahern. But we are assured by the manufacturers that the streamliners have a top speed of 45 miles an hour. And some run is necessary to attain that speed. The older cars, of course, can come nowhere near that."[23]

Ahern was unmoved and issued his own statement:

"I know the officials of the CTA are men of outstanding integrity, and would not for a moment dispute their word as to what the car manufacturers claim. I do, however, reiterate that one of their trolleys was clocked at 55 miles an hour."[24]

Within a day of his testimony, Ahern ordered all motorcycle and squad policemen to "chase and stop" any CTA Green Hornets and trolley buses found to be exceeding the posted speed limit.[25] He told his men to take the names of motormen and record the numbers of their vehicles. Although police were unable to issue citations, cases involving speeding streetcars would be turned over to the CTA. "In some previous cases," Ahern explained, "trolley pilots have been suspended for as much as five days."[26]

He also said that he had eight cases ready to be turned over to the CTA. He planned to compile a report to present to jurors before they completed their findings and made their final recommendations.[27]

CTA employees George Hartwig and Peter Duggan testified at the Inquest as they had done a week earlier as part of the CTA inquest. At that time, both men described watching flagman Charles Kleim standing in the street waving to the approaching trolley. But their stories changed slightly under questioning at the Coroner's Inquest.

Duggan described seeing Kleim standing on the east side of State Street from his vantage point where the trolleys exited the turnaround loop. He also admitted that he was the person who plugged the switch at about 2:40 p.m. when it became clear that the viaduct would remain impassable for streetcar traffic for some time.[28]

When pressed further about Kleim's position, Duggan said he watched Kleim flagging other cars—but his view was obstructed immediately prior to the collision. Duggan also suggested that Manning probably had no idea that he was about to be rerouted and that he had received no previous warning. He was quick to add that more than 200 cars had been safely switched during the four hours prior to the collision.[29]

Hartwig's trolley had just been ushered into the turnaround loop by the signals of Charles Kleim. Like Duggan, Hartwig said he saw Kleim just before the collision:

"I saw the flagman signaling with his hands. I turned and saw the other car coming from the north some distance away. I turned to get instructions from the supervisor, and the next thing I knew, there was a crash and flames all around."[30] Neither Duggan nor Hartwig was looking directly at Kleim at the time of the collision. They were, in fact, in conversation with one another as Duggan explained the details of the short-turn to the motorman. This latest revelation set the stage for the day's most captivating witness.

Next to Charles Kleim, Walter Skonicki had perhaps the best view of the accident. Skonicki had been lying on his living room sofa at the front of his home, which looked out onto State Street and the turnaround.

He was 48 years old, but he looked much older. He was balding, and his face was deeply lined. *The Chicago Defender* described him as "elderly."[31] The Skonicki house had escaped serious damage. A fence in front of the home had caught fire briefly, and some of the exterior paint had bubbled from the intense heat. His daughter lost her car to the flames because it was parked near the turnaround on the east side of State Street.[32]

Skonicki was a sensitive man who had not been prepared for the horrors he had witnessed on May 25. He wept as he described the scene:

"It was horrible—they were hollering and screaming and I couldn't help them."[33]

After he composed himself again, Skonicki was asked about the movements of CTA flagger Charles Kleim.

Skonicki testified that he had watched several cars enter the switch and pass through the turnaround. But his next statement sent reporters scurrying for the phones.

In the seconds just prior to the collision, Skonicki said, ". . . there was no man at the switch. The CTA man was standing on the sidewalk."[34]

Prior to Skonicki's statement, the whereabouts of Charles Kleim had been taken for granted. No other witness had suggested that Kleim had been absent from his post in front of the switch. Now, here was an impartial witness who suggested that the flagger—not the motorman—was to blame for the accident.

Brodie called the chambers to order as the gallery murmured over this latest revelation. Seated next to the attorney she had hired, Mamie Manning dared to hope. Perhaps her husband had not been at fault after all?

Brodie and the Inquest jury approached the revelation with an air of caution. It would likely take more than one witness to convince them that the flagger had been absent from his post. But Skonicki's testimony had been compelling.[35]

Kleim was the last witness to testify that afternoon, and he had some explaining to do. He began by describing his day on May 25:

> I began work that morning at 3:30 o'clock driving a CTA bus. When I finished my customary shift shortly after noon, they had other work for me. I was sent at 2:45 p.m. to the State Street turnaround pocket, where I

reported as a flagman at the switch. I was stationed about four feet north of the switch, close to the southbound rail. Many cars had been flagged down and passed safely into the pocket.[36]

Leonard Bosgarf, attorney for the Manning family, asked about the long hours Kleim had worked that day and the effect it may have had on his ability to do his job.

"Is it true," he asked, "you had been on duty almost continuously for almost 12 hours and you hadn't eaten since 9:00 a.m.?" Kleim said it was true, although in reality he had been at work for more than 15 hours when the accident occurred.[37]

As he had done at the CTA inquest, Kleim described his actions as Manning's trolley came into view. He said he first noticed the trolley when it was about two blocks away.

"When it entered the 6200 block, I started signaling. He kept on coming. It became apparent to me that he was coming with a little speed."[38]

Kleim was reluctant to say how fast he thought the trolley was traveling as it approached the switch. In response to one such question, he declined to speculate as he "had no instruments to estimate speed."[39]

At the CTA inquiry the day after the accident, Kleim had estimated the trolley's speed at 30 miles an hour. That estimate was supported by several motorists whose vehicles were passed by Manning on State Street as he approached the switch. At the same time, CTA chairman Ralph Budd had suggested that the trolley was traveling at a slower speed—"more like 20 mph."[40]

The jurors and attorneys were not happy with what they considered to be Kleim's evasiveness. In order to reconstruct the accident, it was necessary to estimate Manning's speed prior to entering the switch. They continued to assail Kleim with questions about the vehicle's speed. Kleim finally gave in, but his answer surprised everyone. He said that Manning's car appeared to slow down somewhat as he signaled. He continued, saying he believed the car was "moving about 20 miles an hour when it entered the switch."[41]

This new estimate was a full 10 miles an hour less than his original estimate of 30 miles an hour made a week earlier. Kleim seemed to be echoing his boss, who was not a witness to the accident. Budd's estimate came from his belief that a streetcar traveling at 30 miles per hour would have derailed upon entering such a sharp curve. Although

Kleim was adamant in his assertions as to his position at the switch, his new speed estimate cast doubt upon his testimony. Prof. Ahern, jury foreman, told the press after the testimonies had ended, "We are not yet satisfied about where the flagman was."[42]

Neither were reporters. Headlines in the evening editions focused on Skonicki's testimony and raised doubts about Charles Kleim. "Where was Flagger in Streetcar Blast?" asked a headline in the *Chicago Daily News* that afternoon.[43]

A state's attorney suggested that if Chief Ahern could locate more witnesses to support Skonicki's claim, then Kleim might be charged with criminal negligence.[44]

After the morning session, jurors were escorted to motor coaches that had been hired to carry them to the crash site at 62nd Place and State Street. For most of the jurors, it was their first visit to the scene. From the corner of 63rd Street to the turnaround loop to the north, the east side of State Street was unrecognizable. The walls of the tenement at 6241 S. State had collapsed, and four other buildings were hollowed-out shells. Every building from the turnaround to the corner of 63rd was either destroyed or severely damaged.

Emergency crews had restored power to the area within 12 hours. CTA crews had begun replacing downed trolley cable as soon as the last police squadrol carried the last victim to the morgue. By dawn, trolley service had been restored to the area.

After the jurors arrived, police blocked traffic in the northbound lanes to facilitate an investigation of the switch. Jurors were joined by Coroner Brodie, as well as Fire Marshal Mullaney, Chief Ahern, and other police, fire, and transit officials. A CTA official demonstrated the safe operation of a switch, using the switch at 62nd Place as his model. He first retrieved the switch handle from beneath an access panel that was imbedded in the street. He inserted the handle and opened the switch by pulling up on the handle. Then as now, the switch was in perfect working order. He also explained how a switch could be plugged in the open position.

The gas truck still lay in the alleyway between the tracks of the turn-around and what had been the north wall of the tenement at 6241 S. State. The cab of the truck was in ruins. Manning's trolley had done considerable damage. Ironically, it was the cab that appeared to absorb most of the collision—the first tank appeared undamaged, although the impact had separated the semitrailer from the truck.

From the condition of the truck's cab, it was easy to understand why driver Mel Wilson had not survived the collision. But the severity of the damage brought the question of speed back into discussion. Even traveling at 20 miles per hour, a trolley could inflict significant damage to the truck's cab, in spite of the weight of the cargo attached to it. But Manning's trolley had pushed the truck out of the northbound lane of traffic and partially onto the sidewalk in front of the tenement. Kleim's original estimate of 30 miles per hour seemed more plausible.

While viewing the wrecked vehicle, jurors noticed a strange mark on one of the truck's own gas tanks, which had become detached and lay near the wreckage alongside Mel Wilson's lunch pail. The truck—like most semitrailer trucks today—had two supply tanks of gasoline from which it drew its own fuel. Known as "side saddle" tanks by their location on either side of the cab just below the doors, they resemble large, steel drums.[45]

The tank beneath the driver's side had been flattened like a soda can ready for recycling. A ragged shard of metal protruded from where the tank had burst. An indentation was visible running upward at a slight angle from left to right. It measured about four inches wide and was of a size and shape similar to that of the front anti-climber of the Green Hornet.[46]

Most rail vehicles have anti-climbers. On trolleys, anti-climbers are bulky, crescent-shaped steel supports, which conform to the front and rear curve of the vehicle. As their name implies, anti-climbers prevent errant trolleys or other rail vehicles from climbing one another in a collision.

In extreme cases, a streetcar or train might strike a vehicle at high speed, causing a phenomenon known as "telescoping." Telescoping refers to an instance in which the frame of one vehicle climbs another at high speed, causing successive sections of the lead vehicle to crumple dramatically, as in closing the chambers of an extended telescope.[47]

Under the right circumstances, anti-climbers could serve as a sort of battering ram, inflicting serious damage on a vehicle of lesser size and mass. On Green Hornets, they were cosmetically hidden behind long, riveted plates inches above the car's small bumper.

In need of a comparison, police officers were dispatched into State Street to flag down the first Green Hornet to pass the location. Meanwhile, two fire department brass in their Class A uniforms lumbered toward the entrance of the turnaround as they carried the gas tank between them.

By that time, police had managed to stop a Green Hornet just in front of the switch. While bewildered passengers looked on, the fire officials held the crumpled tank against the trolley's front anti-climber. Like the cast of a footprint made in plaster of paris, the anti-climber and the indentation were a visual match.[48]

The entourage returned to the truck, inspecting both of the four-thousand-gallon tanks and their trailers. Incredibly, both tanks had somehow maintained their structural integrity. Neither crumpled significantly during the fire nor burst like a special effect in a disaster movie. The rear tank was completely intact, though its cargo had been washed away by firefighters. At first glance, the front tank appeared as sound as its partner. But on closer inspection, jurors noticed a hole about ten inches long at a point just behind the cab. Mullaney surmised that the hole was made by a portion of the trolley that broke off during the collision. It was from this seemingly innocuous breach in the tank's skin that gasoline had escaped and flowed across State Street.[49]

This latest evidence caused Mullaney to revise his original theory. He abandoned the notion that the initial fire was caused by downed trolley cables or the truck's muffler. He now advanced the idea that gasoline from the flattened supply tank ignited on impact, causing the initial WHOOSH described by eyewitnesses, including Kleim and Skonicki. Fire from this explosion blew through the interior of the trolley like smoke drawn through a cigar, causing passengers to stampede toward the rear of the car.

Mullaney went on to say that, in his opinion, the burning gasoline from the supply tank "probably" killed the passengers on board the trolley.[50]

Interviewed throughout the investigation, Mullaney seemed oblivious to eyewitness reports of passengers struggling within the car for three or four minutes after the collision.

Earlier in the week, the *Chicago Daily News* ran an article that quoted a Dr. Israel Davidson, who suggested that death had come quickly for passengers on board the streetcar. Most died not from burns but from asphyxiation and shock. One breath of the superheated air within the trolley very likely caused the passengers' lungs to collapse. Such a scenario, though grim in itself, might have been more comforting to the families of victims.[51]

Taken one way, the fire marshal seemed to answer with compassion for victims' families—suggesting that death was swift with little struggle and no time to react. Taken another way, however, his words seemed to deflect attention away from the pile-up at the rear doors. Further investigations later in the day would change his mind for good.

While the entourage examined the accident scene, they were accosted by an elderly man named Judson Christmas, who said he had witnessed the accident. Christmas was not quoted in newspapers, and he had not given an official statement to police. He said he had worked as a furniture salesman in the building at 6247 S. State, which had been completely destroyed by the fire. Christmas had lived in the upper floor of that building and was now homeless.

According to Christmas, he had seen Peter Duggan plug the switch earlier in the afternoon, but just prior to the accident, he was certain that no one was at the switch. In the week following the accident, Christmas said he tried to tell his story at CTA headquarters but had been turned away. Police took his statement at the scene, and he was added to the list of witnesses at the Inquest's next session.[52]

The entourage departed the scene in the late afternoon and continued on to the car barn at 77th and Vincennes. Inside the barn, jurors and officials were able to view the burned-out remains of PCC No. 7078. The interior was positively skeletal.

The front of the trolley had been severely damaged as well. Above the anti-climber, the entire façade had caved inward, which pinned Manning in his seat.

Examination of the car revealed that William Liddell had set the door levers to open. But jurors needed a concrete explanation as to why the doors did not immediately comply.[53]

Since the rear doors were used exclusively by boarding passengers, they opened inward. This proved to be a major design flaw in the Hornets, sealing the fate of those passengers trapped inside.

Chicago history was rife with stories of doors that opened inward to public buildings. Most notable was the tragic 1903 fire at Chicago's Iroquois Theater in which more than six hundred people had died. Many of the bodies were found piled before exit doors that opened inward and could not be forced open due to the crush of a panicking crowd. An ordinance was passed making it mandatory for all public buildings to install "fire doors" that opened outward and expedited exit in case of emergency. It stood to reason that the same principle should apply to public conveyances, as well.

Using an undamaged trolley of the same design, jurors examined the rear doors and observed while Mullaney conducted an impromptu test. The fire marshal stood on the inside of a Green Hornet and leaned against one of its rear doors. On the outside, CTA chief mechanical engineer Stanley Forsythe did his best to open the door. He was unsuccessful. "It doesn't take much pressure to keep this door from opening," remarked Mullaney.[54]

Juror James S. Baker, director of research for Northwestern University's Traffic Institute, participated in another test that showed that when pressure was applied to the inside of a door, it could not be opened from the inside or the outside.[55]

Captain Ahern demonstrated that if two persons tried to exit an open door at the same time, it was possible to force the doors shut, preventing further exit by anyone.[56]

Further investigation evoked a clearer picture of what had transpired at the rear doors. Even with the levers set to open, pressure exerted by the passengers against the doors prevented them from opening automatically. That same pressure made it impossible for passengers to open the doors using their fingers. It also prevented any potential rescuers from opening the door from the outside.

Jurors next examined the rear windows through which most survivors scrambled to safety. In spite of the fact that one of the windows was not bolted and could have opened outward, there was no evidence that the unbolted window was ever opened. In the panic, both had remained shut.

Upon examining these windows, Professor Ahern remarked that it was "miraculous that anyone got out of the car."[57]

Before departing the car barn, Brodie gathered the jurors. It had been a productive, revealing day, but there were still many other witnesses set to testify. The coroner reminded jurors that they had not yet heard testimony from survivors of the crash, many of whom were still recuperating in area hospitals. He also urged them to hold off on making any decisions or developing biases before all information had been presented and all witnesses had been heard. With that, Brodie continued the Inquest until June 20 so as to give survivors more time to recover from their injuries and testify before the Inquest.

Chapter EIGHT

While Traffic Chief Michael Ahern was creating awareness about trolley speed, several members of the City Council began to wage war on the gas trucks. Alderman George Kells, who chaired the Committee on Traffic and Public Safety, called a meeting to discuss passing an ordinance to restrict gas haulage in the city. Kells named a subcommittee of six aldermen whose primary purpose was to draft an ordinance to restrict the routes followed by gas trucks through city streets.[1]

Other big cities had regulations in place that controlled the movement of bulk gasoline tankers within city limits. New York, for instance, had an ordinance restricting any truck from carrying in excess of 2,500 gallons of gas along the most-trafficked streets.

"I'm going to get in touch with other cities to examine their rules and regulations for gasoline-hauling trucks," said Kells. "We want the best advice on this subject we can get. The trucking interests have fought against most of our ordinances regulating freight traffic and load limits."[2]

But the true standard-bearer in the fight to restrict gasoline haulage wasn't even on Kells's committee. John Hoellen was still in his first term as alderman of the 47th Ward, which primarily encompassed the north-side Ravenswood community. His father had preceded him as an alderman representing the same ward more than a decade earlier.

Hoellen was already establishing himself as a political maverick within the Council. In fact, Hoellen clashed with his colleagues in several respects. The most obvious was his political affiliation. Like his father before him, Hoellen was a Republican. He would be elected and re-elected to his post a total of seven times, and in a career spanning 28 years, he was sometimes the only Republican alderman in a Council run by Chicago's Democratic machine.[3]

Although he crossed the aisle many times during his career to collaborate with Democratic colleagues, Hoellen was sometimes the lone voice of dissent in the Council chambers. He was a particular nemesis of Richard J. Daley, Chicago's Napoleonic mayor and boss of its political machine. Daley called Hoellen "the phoniest fellow who ever came into this Council."[4]

On June 8, 1950, while the Coroner's Inquest stood in recess, Hoellen told reporters that he was drafting an ordinance "banning gasoline tank trailers" of the double-trailer type involved in the May 25 accident. He said he planned to introduce the ordinance at the next Council meeting.[5]

Hoellen called tank trucks "an unnecessary hazard," and pointed out that cities like New York prohibited them. One recommendation modified from the New York plan involved setting a limit of 3,000 gallons as the top tank capacity. Hoellen also suggested that those tanks be further divided into compartments not to exceed 500 gallons.[6]

At the time, there was no regulation limiting the size of tanks for haulage of gasoline in Chicago. City ordinances did require compartments of no more than 600 gallons, but only for those trucks making deliveries and operating exclusively within city limits. The Sprout & Davis truck was exempt from the law. Hoellen believed this loophole was equally culpable in the streetcar deaths.

"I'm convinced the fire would have been less costly in property and human life if the whole 4,000 gallons on that tank truck had not been spilled."[7]

Other New York codes recommended by Hoellen included limiting gasoline delivery only to the hours of minimal street congestion. That meant the hours between 7 p.m. and 7 a.m. He cited safety regulations recommended by the Interstate Commerce Commission, which stated that large tank trucks ought to be routed away from congested streets, crowds, viaducts, tunnels, dangerous crossings, and trolley tracks.

Also suggested was the creation of a mandatory physical and mental examination for all drivers of gas trucks. Upon passing these examinations, drivers would become certified to operate such vehicles.[8]

Hoellen presented his plan to the Council on June 14, and it was referred to the special subcommittee for consideration.[9] If his arguments were not convincing enough, they were fueled by an incident that occurred the following day. On June 15, a gas truck was involved in a single-vehicle accident in the village of Northlake, a suburb just a few miles west of Chicago.

The driver of the truck, Walter A. James, was traveling eastbound on North Avenue when he had to swerve suddenly to avoid a pedestrian who had emerged unexpectedly from a parked truck. James lost control of his vehicle, and the truck rode up onto the center parkway of North Avenue. Ironically, the truck driven by Jones was of the identical double-trailer design involved in the May 25 accident. It was also owned by the Sprout & Davis Company.

When the truck climbed over the median, the rear trailer became unhitched and turned over, causing the tank to spill its contents all over busy North Avenue. By some minor miracle, the gasoline did not ignite. Fire crews arrived and managed to wash the tank's contents—between 3,500 and 4,000 gallons of gasoline—down a sewer drain. The sewer line emptied into nearby Addison Creek.

About two hours later, fire officials were summoned once again. Addison Creek was on fire! Apparently, a passing motorist had tossed a cigarette into the creek. Gasoline had pooled on the creek's surface and caught fire. Within minutes the surface of the creek on both sides of the flashpoint was set ablaze for the length of a mile. Flames rose as high as 30 feet and sent residents who lived along the creek's edge scurrying into the streets.

Firefighters managed to suffocate the flames by employing the fine mist spray technique used in the May 25 fire. They were aided by rainfall later in the afternoon. No one was injured and no houses were damaged, but four bridges over the creek were destroyed.[10]

Hoellen referenced the Northlake fire when he addressed the special subcommittee the following week, as evidence that accidents involving double-bottom tankers were still occurring and likely to continue. In addition to members of the special subcommittee, the meeting was also attended by police and fire officials, as well as representatives of the gasoline trucking industry and trucking union.[11]

Once Hoellen's proposed ordinance was read, the special subcommittee chair, Alderman Emil Pacini, asked the trucking reps if they had any objections. Both asked for more time to research the proposal.

Hoellen was overtly opposed by one member of the subcommittee—Alderman Reginald Dubois of the 9th Ward, who owned a filling station. DuBois complained that to accommodate Hoellen's plans for late-night fuel deliveries, he would lose money paying attendants to stay on after regular hours. It would also force truck drivers to work evenings. Fred M. Tiedt, president of Local 705 of the truckers union, said he saw a potential problem with contract agreements between the truckers union and gas suppliers.[12]

Hoellen replied that in New York, gasoline suppliers managed to make all of their deliveries in the evening using only about one-third of the trucks that they used during the daytime. Nighttime deliveries were actually more efficient and cost effective.[13]

Chief John Fenn of the Fire Prevention Bureau read evidence that supported his belief that compartmented tankers were "less hazardous" than undivided tanks.[14]

Robert J. Nolan, an assistant corporation counsel in attendance, suggested that the special subcommittee had been provided with sufficient evidence by Alderman Hoellen and others to rule on the ordinance. The trucking interests said they would be ready to make their own recommendations in about ten days. Alderman Pacini adjourned the meeting until after July 4.[15]

While the Inquest lay in recess, Chief Ahern kept the heat on. His motorcycle patrolmen continued to clock Green Hornets on Chicago streets and record their speeds. Ahern also forced the hand of CTA officials, asking what recommendations they were making in light of the accident and subsequent investigations.

The CTA decided to respond to inquiries made by Ahern and several others at the reconvened Inquest on June 20. It was decided that Ralph Budd would testify on behalf of the company. Budd was the first witness called that day, and he remained on the stand for nearly 90 minutes answering questions from jurors and attorneys as well as presenting the CTA's carefully crafted response.

He began by describing the tragedy as an occurrence that came about through "a chain of circumstances almost impossible to duplicate." One by one, Budd enumerated each contributing factor, beginning with the flooded viaduct at 63rd and State streets, which necessitated southbound traffic to use the turnaround at 62nd Place.[16]

He explained how to accomplish this movement by opening the switch located in the southbound lanes of traffic. He insisted that a flagger was in place to direct streetcar movement, adding that 220 cars had been properly switched in this manner throughout the afternoon.

Regarding the actions of motorman Paul Manning, Budd testified that it was Manning's failure to comply with the flagger's directions—

as well as his apparent disregard for procedure when approaching a switch—that brought about the collision with the gas truck. Budd allowed that although Manning entered the switch at "a high rate of speed," he refused to budge on his 20-mile-per-hour estimate.[17]

Budd also responded to the CTA policy regarding a trolley's speed when approaching a facing switch—a subject of some controversy at the June 1 session of the Inquest. Adding to the comments made by CTA attorney Kelly at that session, Budd explained that the CTA policy did not require motormen to reduce speed to a required limit. Rather, motormen were required to reduce speed sufficiently so as to be able to determine whether a switch was open and to be able to stop immediately, if necessary.

Manning had been a motorman for four years. He had what Budd described as a "good" record and he was in good health. Budd said that the rules regarding hiring and training employees were constantly changing, but the company exercised integrity in both regards. Methods were always being employed to "improve the discipline of our operators."[18]

According to Budd, the Green Hornets "embodied the best design features of 12 to 15 years of study," and "represent(ed) the joint effort of the best minds in the industry."[19]

"But it wasn't perfect," he admitted. He offered that the best safety devices should operate only when they are needed. "We're in constant search for improvements, such as exits that will work in an emergency but won't operate when they shouldn't. We're studying leaving the safety bars off one window on each side."[20]

Budd was asked if the rear doors could be operated even if the trolley pole had been disconnected. This question was posed in response to a statement made by Charles Kleim, who said he "lowered the trolley pole" immediately after the collision. Budd explained that the doors were in no way dependent upon the trolley (pole), in that they operated from batteries.

He was also questioned about the rear windows through which a majority of the survivors escaped. Why was one of the windows always latched? Budd did not immediately answer this question, but he sent a written reply to juror Lyndon F. Wilson that explained "hazards which would prevail if both rear windows could be opened."[21] He noted that several large cities used PCCs that had stationary rear windows, including Philadelphia, St. Louis, and Pittsburgh.

Budd was most sensitive to questions regarding the proposal of speed limits imposed on streetcars. He explained that instead of imposing a direct limit on its operators, the CTA emphasized that motormen operate within speed parameters that elicited safe operation. He believed that imposing a fixed limit on motormen might, in fact, "encourage speeding."[22]

Budd was willing to work with the recommendations offered by the Inquest jurors, but he ended his testimony with a plea to exercise great caution in tampering with established practices.

At least a dozen other witnesses gave testimony. Two CTA supervisors, both of whom were stationed along Manning's route on May 25, testified that they had alerted all streetcars passing their stations that they were to be re-routed at the turnaround pocket near 62nd Place. One of the supervisors, Vernon Touranjeau, who was stationed at 51st Street, said he recalled his exchange with Manning specifically. Manning had a habit of chewing gum and would wave a stick of gum at the supervisor "in a form of salutation" as he passed the supervisor's corner.[23]

Four passengers who had been aboard the PCC gave their accounts of the moments on board the trolley just prior to and following the collision. Eunice Savage, who boarded the car at 57th Street, said she got up from her seat at about 61st Street preparing to disembark at 63rd Street. She stepped down onto the treaded step in front of the center door. Looking out through the side window of the blinker door, she noticed a supervisor waving his hands wildly just as the car passed his position. Immediately after that, the car jolted into the switch and Savage was thrown to the floor. The flow of passengers forced her to the rear of the car. She recalled exiting through one of the rear doors.[24]

Arleen Franzen, who had watched her friend Carol Rudenga perish in the flames, testified that she had taken a seat opposite the center doors. Like Eunice Savage, she was thrown to the floor and trampled. She escaped through one of the rear windows, adding that a "CTA man wearing a tan jacket" had helped her to safety. This supported Charles Kleim's claim that he had helped several passengers exit through the rear windows until the heat became too intense and drove him away. She estimated the car's speed to be about 30 miles per hour.[25]

Edward White told jurors he had boarded the car at 22nd Street and found a seat opposite conductor William Liddell on the right side near the rear exits. His position did not afford him a view through the windshield of the movements of Charles Kleim. He estimated the trolley's speed at between 30 and 35 miles per hour. He told how he tried to kick a glass pane out of one of the rear doors, which caused the injury to his leg. But one of the doors swung open, allowing him to escape.[26]

Chief Ahern read a statement given by passenger Ben Head, who was still recuperating from severe burns at Provident Hospital. Head stated that he boarded the car at 34th Street. He described seeing a man in a CTA cap and blue shirt standing about three feet from the switch and "waving violently with both hands" as he tried to stop the car. Head estimated the car's speed at "around 30 mph." He exited through the rear window.[27]

One of the most controversial testimonies came from passenger John Seawright, who told the Inquest he boarded the car at 46th Street. In newspaper accounts, Seawright said he was a friend of William Liddell and was engaged in conversation with him just before the collision. In fact, he told one paper that he meant to exit at 61st Street, but missed his stop because he was talking with Liddell. He told the Inquest that he was seated next to Liddell and was able to escape by pulling at the rubber inserts in the rear doors, causing one of them to open enough for him to squeeze through. He estimated the car's speed at about 30 miles per hour.[28] He also told the Inquest that he telephoned Liddell's wife later that evening to let her know her husband was safe.[29]

When he testified later that day, William Liddell denied knowing Seawright. He said he had boarded at 61st Street, not 46th Street.[30]

Liddell's testimony was largely the same version he gave at the CTA inquest on May 25 with a few exceptions. Liddell told the jury that the trolley made a stop at 61st Street, less than two blocks before the collision. He may have been mistaken. No other passenger mentioned a stop at 61st Street, and several eyewitnesses remarked at their surprise when the trolley did not make a stop there. Nevertheless, Liddell said it was so, and he was not challenged on the stand by any juror, attorney, or the coroner.

After stopping at 61st Street, he told the Inquest that the car continued on as usual. As they neared the turnaround, Liddell said he became aware of a buzzing sound, which meant that the emergency brake had been applied. All at once, he found himself on the floor and was trampled by passengers stampeding toward the rear of the car. He managed to get to his feet, shouting to passengers to stand away from the rear doors while he set the levers to open.

Here, Liddell added a significant detail not given during his May

26 testimony. After he set the levers, the rear doors opened briefly, allowing several passengers to exit. This revelation was substantiated by the small number of survivors who insisted they had exited through the rear doors, including Seawright, Edward White, Eunice Savage, and Mary Pokorney.[31]

The doors were forced closed once again as passengers rushed to the rear en masse with flames trailing them. Liddell told jurors that after his escape, he was driven by an acquaintance to a doctor's office. He also said he spent the night at the home of that acquaintance, but he still would not reveal that person's identity.[32]

Robert Mitchell, the witness who had fainted after viewing photos of the accident at the June 1 session, was expected to testify and share information regarding the speed of the vehicle and the whereabouts of flagman Charles Kleim. Mitchell was traveling in a car with three other men, including passenger Robert C. Lockinour and driver George Alsup, Jr. Lockinour testified that Manning's streetcar passed Alsup's car between 61st Street and the scene of the accident. He estimated that Alsup was traveling between 25 and 30 miles per hour when the trolley passed them.[33]

He estimated the distance between Alsup's vehicle and the trolley to have been about 50 feet. He also said that he saw a flagman signaling trolleys. He said this individual was standing midway between the curb and the southbound track.

Alsup also testified, giving essentially the same account as Lockinour. As the two other passengers were expected to give similar testimony as Lockinour and Alsup, neither was called to the stand. After all he had been through, Robert Mitchell never had to testify.[34]

Also addressed at the Inquest were the controversial comments made by eyewitness Walter Skonicki at the June 1 session. Skonicki had left the jury conflicted as to the whereabouts of Charles Kleim after the witness said he saw Kleim "standing on the sidewalk" just prior to the collision. Paul Molette, who was seated in a car parked on the west side of State Street just before the accident, gave testimony that seemed to support Skonicki's claim. Molette told the jury that he saw a flagman directing cars into the turnaround pocket at 62nd Place. Shortly before the collision, Molette left the car and crossed over to the east side of State Street. As he reached the door to a tavern, he glanced to his left and noticed the flagger leaving his post and walking to the east side of the street to talk to a supervisor. After entering the tavern, Molette immediately heard the sound of the collision.

However, in a memo to CTA attorney James O. Dwight, CTA attorney R. F. Kelly wrote that Molette "…appeared to be under the influence of liquor during the time he was testifying." He suggested that Molette's account should be considered unreliable.[35]

Also testifying was Judson Christmas, the elderly furniture salesman who ambushed the Inquest jury at the crash scene on June 1, stating that he saw no one at the switch at the time of the accident.

Christmas faltered on the stand, however. He said he was walking on the east side of State Street about 150 feet north of the accident. Contrary to his June 1 claim, he said he did see a man standing in the middle of the street, but he didn't know what he was doing. As with Molette, his testimony was not given much credence.[36]

At the request of Coroner A. L. Brodie, CTA attorney James O. Dwight read into the record a statement regarding the health of motorman Paul Manning. Dwight noted that Manning's last illness was recorded on April 6, 1948, when the motorman missed three workdays. The nature of the illness was not indicated in the statement. Manning had been given a furlough a few weeks prior to the accident in order to visit his ailing mother in Mississippi. During the furlough, Manning missed worked from April 25 through May 14, 1950. With the exception of his regularly scheduled off days, Manning had worked every day since his return on May 15.[37]

As Ralph Budd had done earlier at the CTA press conference on May 26, Dwight read into the record a statement regarding Manning's performance record, specifically with regard to his ten previous accidents.[38]

Dwight also addressed CTA policy regarding flooded underpasses. In a letter submitted by a Mr. H. L. Howell, superintendent of ways and structures of the Chicago Transit Authority, Dwight explained that streetcar service was generally suspended whenever standing water reached a level of just four inches above the rails. On May 25, two storms passed through the area. The first storm, which occurred at about 2:00 p.m., caused the initial flooding of the underpass at 63rd and State streets, causing trolley traffic to be re-routed into the turnaround pocket. A second storm followed between 3:30 and 4:00 p.m., bringing more rain. According to Howell's letter, pumps were put in place inside the underpass at about 5:00 p.m. The pumps were still operating just after 6:30 p.m. when power was lost due to wires' being downed by the accident.[39]

Ironically, Howell explained that the underpass was nearly ready for travel. Trolley service would have resumed within another 15 or 20 minutes.

Chief Ahern also presented his much-anticipated report on streetcar speeds. Since June 1, he had ordered his motorcycle and squad police officers to follow random Green Hornets and record their speeds. Nearly three weeks later, Ahern's patrolmen had recorded 100 Green Hornets in various parts of the city traveling at a speed of 35 miles per hour or faster. Almost one-third of these were clocked at 40 miles per hour or greater. One trolley's speed was reported at 47 miles per hour. The majority of the speeding trolleys were observed on the north side of the city on Western and Broadway avenues.[40]

The report seemed to vindicate the Traffic Chief's claim that some trolley motormen were operating their vehicles at unsafe speeds.

After Ahern's testimony, Brodie continued the Inquest until June 29, at which time the jury was expected to report its findings and make its recommendations.

Chapter
NINE

The Coroner's Inquest jury met for a final session on June 29, and presented its conclusions based on evidence presented in the two previous sessions. In addition, the jury presented a list of recommendations covering trolley travel, gasoline haulage, and other mitigating factors.

At the start, the jury announced that the May 25 crash between a Green Hornet streetcar and a gasoline tanker truck was determined to be accidental—the result of a dizzying number of factors. Professor J. J. Ahern read a list of seven conclusions.

As Ralph Budd had done earlier in the Inquest, Ahern began with the flooded viaduct at 63rd and State streets. The rains and an inadequate drainage system had made the short-turning of trolleys necessary via the turnaround loop at 62nd Place.[1]

Paul Manning, the streetcar motorman, either did not know or did not realize that he was to make the short-turn, and he entered the switch at an excessive speed.[2]

Mel Wilson's gas truck conformed to all regulations and with respect to all agencies. Manning's trolley had struck the truck's supply tank, which split open. The tank contained about 40 gallons of gasoline, which ignited on impact. The sudden jolt caused the semitrailer containing the first tank to ride up onto the rear of the truck. A portion of the truck's frame tore a gash in the tank and gasoline immediately began to pour out and flow along the grade of the street. The gasoline was ignited by flames from the initial fire. The second tank was undamaged, and its vents functioned properly, preventing a second explosion.[3]

Based on survivor testimony, the jury surmised that "a typical panic ensued" on board the trolley, as passengers escaping the flames rushed to the rear exits. The rear doors were forced shut as passengers exerted pressure on them.[4]

Recalling the tests made at the car barn earlier in the Inquest, jurors were adamant in their criticism of the PCC's safety failures.

"It is the opinion of the jury that the emergency facilities on the so-called President's Conference Committee cars of the CTA are entirely inadequate. The doors will not open if there is pressure on the inside. Furthermore, if the car should turn over on its right side, all exit facilities are blocked except that provided by the rear windows."[5]

The jury also acknowledged indirectly the work of Chief Michael Ahern, suggesting that trolley speed was "sometimes excessive for city traffic conditions."[6]

With regard to gasoline haulage, jurors acknowledged the need for bulk deliveries in a city of Chicago's size. Although Alderman Hoellen did not address the Inquest, his efforts were well documented in the papers. Jurors appeared to disagree with Hoellen's proposal to restrict large-volume tankers. "At the outset, the jury agrees that it is impossible to determine the quantity that would be a safe amount of gasoline." Bulk deliveries could be made "under control and careful supervision of the local authorities as to route, construction, and time of day."[7]

The jury also disagreed with the prospect of night deliveries, calling them "not possible," although no reason for the impracticality of the plan was given. Rather, it suggested that deliveries be made at a time "when the exposure to traffic will be at a minimum."[8]

Jurors made a final conclusion regarding Paul Manning. "The motorman of this street car had been involved in ten accidents during the preceding sixteen months. It would seem that this record would have warranted special attention."[9]

Following their conclusions, Prof. Ahern read a list of 12 recommendations:

> 1. An intensive effort should be made to provide adequate drainage for the underpass south of Sixty-third and State Street, and all others subject to flooding, particularly where the street is used by street car or bus lines. With increasing volumes of traffic, these will become a still more serious source of delays and an indirect cause of accidents. It is recognized that the underpass drainage is only part of a large sewer problem, in which the main obstacles are not technical, but financial. This emphasizes the need for a new approach to a general situation which has been becoming more and more aggravating for a quarter of a century.

It is suggested that sincere consideration be given to joining water disposal with water supply so that both may be financed by the water user through meter payments instead of from general funds;

2. All transit vehicles should be equipped with an emergency exit or exits on the left side as is now common in aircraft and school buses;

3. The doors of all transit vehicles should be designed to remain in the open position when opened for emergency purposes. They should also be so designed as to open regardless of internal pressure;

4. As soon as practicable, remove the permanent fastenings from the left rear window of the PCC cars so that both rear windows can be swung open in an emergency;

5. Consideration should be given to a replacement of the present bars on street car windows with devices easily removable in the event of an emergency;

6. Before and whenever any manually operated track switch in a street is blocked open, a temporary warning signal should be placed between the rails beyond the switch. This should have a target area of at least two square feet by day and illumination by night equal to at least two pot torches or flares. These signals should be so constructed that they will do little damage to a vehicle should they be struck. Emergency and cruising supervisory vehicles of the CTA should carry such signal equipment. In locations where this procedure is frequently necessary, consideration should be given to a permanent installation of a flasher light to warn both traffic and the operator of the street car;

7. Special distinctive and conspicuous belts with shoulder straps should be provided for all flagmen who work in city streets. These should be reflectorized for night operation. Emergency and supervisory cruising vehicles of the CTA should carry such equipment;

8. All transit operators should have a complete physical examination at least once every six months;

9. The CTA should re-study its entire accident prevention program for operators, giving special attention to its methods of handling accident repeaters, to make use of the most modern methods of dealing with operators who have become conspicuous because of their accident records;

10. Legislation should be enacted which will bring all operators of street cars and trolley buses under the same speed limitations as those applying to the operators of motor vehicles;

11. All tank trucks should conform to standards comparable to those published by the National Fire Protection Association;

12. Bulk deliveries of gasoline or liquids of comparable hazard in amounts of over 1,200 gallons should be made only over routes designated by the City authorities and only between the hours of midnight and 7:00 a.m., with the exception of Sunday, when no bulk deliveries shall be made. This restriction should not apply to tanks which are divided into compartments not exceeding 600 gallons each.[10]

The jury concluded its recommendations with an honest, heartfelt appeal to strongly consider its findings:

> The foregoing is submitted with the sincere hope that it will be useful in preventing a repetition of this horrible disaster. It is recognized that the problem presented in transporting hazardous materials and large numbers of people on the streets of the City is not one which can be easily solved in a short period of time. The Jury urges that the City of Chicago make a thorough and long range study of all the ramifications of this situation so as to provide a permanent, practical and safe solution to the problem.[11]

Considering the intense drama that had preceded it, the jury's report made for a disappointing denouement. The rhetoric was bland and empirical. As the final word in one of the worst disasters in the city's history, the report should have delivered a resounding spank to the Transit Authority. Instead, its conclusions lacked any sense of moral outrage. Its recommendations were broad and nonspecific, giving a tremendous amount of latitude in which the CTA could operate. Moreover, it failed to adequately and conclusively address key issues in the case. The list was long.

THE SWITCH—In spite of the fact that more than two hundred trolleys were safely turned on the afternoon of May 25, 1950, the system for switching trolleys was deeply flawed. Though publicly frowned upon, the dangerous practice of plugging the switch was clearly tolerated within the company and contributed as much to the deaths that day as Manning's inattentiveness. Had the switch not been plugged, Manning's trolley would have continued through the closed switch and on to the safety island less than 100 yards away. Passengers would have been inconvenienced and Manning probably would have received a slap on the wrist. But nobody would have died.

MANNING—The jury was not specific as to how many accidents in a particular time frame were enough to label a motorman as "suspicious" or a "risk." As the CTA did not appear to have a specific total in mind, it was within the purview of the jury to make such a recommendation. Manning's high total should have been a red flag at the car barn. During the same period, Charles Kleim was involved in only four accidents compared to Manning's ten.[12] Had some CTA safeguard been in effect—mandatory completion of a seminar akin to traffic safety school after five accidents in one year—it might have been the wake-up call Manning needed and made him more attentive that day.

KLEIM—If Charles Kleim was wearing a tan windbreaker, as Arleen Franzen testified at the Coroner's Inquest, that simple addition of "civilian" clothing to his CTA uniform might have been enough to confuse Paul Manning as he approached the switch. From the motorman's vantage point, Kleim might very well have looked like an out-of-place pedestrian who was trying to board the streetcar in the middle of the street.

Kleim had been on the job for more than 15 hours. Although he took a lunch break while running his bus route earlier in the day, there is no mention that he took one during his four hours at the switch. When Walter Skonicki testified that he saw Kleim standing on the sidewalk across the street, Kleim may have jogged over to the supervisor asking for a bathroom break or for an estimate as to when he would finally be relieved.

If it happened, that brief absence from the switch from the time that George Hartwig's streetcar entered the turnaround and Manning's car entered the 6200 block of State Street might have been the only time Manning was looking directly at the switch. It could have been enough to convince the motorman that he would continue on to 63rd Street unmolested.

COMMUNICATION—Trolleys were never fitted with radios. All communication was handed down from the barns to the supervisors to the motormen. If every member along the chain performed his job with integrity, it was an effective system. But if even one of the supervisors along Manning's route was derelict in his duty, it supports the assertion that Manning wasn't expecting a flagger at 62nd Place.

THE TROLLEY—In the face of imminent danger, how do you get passengers out of a streetcar if all of the exits on the right side of the vehicle are blocked?

In the best of circumstances, questions like the above are resolved on the drawing board a decade before vehicles ever go online. Engineers are trained to consider all of the "what-ifs"—those persistent, nagging scenarios containing every possible calamity—and wed them to reasonable solutions. If the PCC was such a versatile and reliable vehicle, why then was there no reliable secondary exit that was clearly marked and effective in discharging passengers when the primary exits were rendered useless?

Ralph Budd was a good engineer in his day and a self-described daily rider of CTA vehicles. On one of his excursions aboard a Green Hornet, did the meticulous railroad man ever consider an answer to the question? Although nothing like the accident of May 25, 1950 had ever occurred, the question should have been asked by someone and a solution should have been made policy.

Within a year of the accident the CTA added several safety features to the Green Hornets. In spite of Ralph Budd's fears against such measures, engineers installed levers that allowed passengers to open doors in an emergency. An ad campaign demonstrated how to operate the levers, which were conspicuously located. Few if any passengers took advantage of the feature and opened the doors for their own amusement in non-emergency situations.

The CTA also removed all of the safety bars along the right side of the vehicles, which allowed more space for passengers to exit through a side window if the situation called for it. CTA engineers, however, refused to completely remove the bars from the left side of the cars, arguing as they had in the past that such an action would cause injuries to passengers who were foolish enough to stick their arms and heads out of the windows as the cars passed in close proximity to one another.

Bars were removed from several windows on the left side. These windows were fitted with "kick-out" frames that could be knocked out in an emergency. Both rear windows were also fitted with the frames, which gave passengers at least four additional exits in an emergency situation.[13]

The additions were not perfect. There were still no doors on the left side of the cars. One characteristic of the May 25 accident was the fact that the gasoline fire, already tearing its way through the trolley, became quickly concentrated along the right side of the vehicle. Within seconds, all three exits were rendered impassable.

The CTA engineers saw the addition of a doorway on the left side as impractical. The PCCs were adaptable, but they had their limits. The kick-out windows were a compromise.

Collisions involving Green Hornets continued throughout the first half of the decade even as progressively more of the vehicles were decommissioned in favor of motor and trolley buses.

In August 1952, a trolley went through a switch that had been left open at Ashland Avenue and 63rd Street. The trolley hopped the track and slid laterally into the safety island, injuring six people who had been waiting to board the car. Police had no idea why the switch had been left open.[14]

On December 28, 1953, 23 persons were injured when a Green Hornet broadsided a Standard Oil tanker truck at 29th and State streets. The trolley severely crumpled the side of the tanker, cutting a large gash in its skin. The driver of the truck told authorities that he had only moments before made his last delivery of the day. Thankfully, the tank was empty.[15]

On November 15, 1954, three people were killed and 35 were injured when a Trans-America Van Service truck collided with a Green Hornet on Western Avenue near 61st Street. The truck's driver, who failed a field sobriety test, was charged with driving while intoxicated as well as reckless homicide.

The driver said he swerved to avoid hitting a female pedestrian who darted out in front of his truck. His truck hit the safety island and then crossed into the southbound lanes where he collided with the trolley. Two passengers and the trolley motorman were killed.[16]

In February 1952, more than 20 months after the May 25, 1950, accident, a Green Hornet traveling on Washington Boulevard near North Western Station emerged from a viaduct and struck a double-bottom tank truck at Franklin just one block west of the Loop.

The trolley derailed, and several passengers were injured.

The tanker rolled over in the crash, and its entire cargo—several thousand gallons of milk—washed across the intersection.

Nearly two years after the accident the clumsy, double-rig tankers were still hauling liquids—both hazardous and harmless—over nearly every manner of city streets and at any time of the day.

The milk truck accident prompted an editorial from the editors of *The Chicago Tribune*. Under the heading "It Might Have Been Gasoline Again," the editors praised the CTA for the safety measures added to the trolleys in the year following the May 25 accident, and they lambasted the City Council for its inability to significantly restrict gasoline haulage.

"The CTA obviously doesn't like to burn up its passengers. The City Council is on record in favor of another holocaust."[17]

Debate over Alderman Hoellen's ordinance persisted through the rest of 1950 and nearly all of the following year. Six months after the creation of the subcommittee, Hoellen's ordinance still had not been approved. The trucking industry went so far as to submit their 1951 schedule of routes for tank trucks—as they did every year—without any significant variation from the schedules they had used prior to the accident.

The action infuriated Hoellen, who chided the special subcommittee for failing to act on the proposal. It took another nine months for the subcommittee members to agree on a plan and recommend it to the City Council. Fifteen months of deliberation and compromise had severely decimated Hoellen's proposal, making it almost unrecognizable. Left out were the proposed ban on gasoline deliveries of more than 3,000 gallons, as well as the restriction of all deliveries to nighttime. Also gone was the proposed ban on double rig trailers.[18]

The proposal that reached the Council was thoroughly emasculated and contained only three points—none of which contained much bite:

> 1. Gasoline trucks would be required to follow routes to be determined by traffic engineers;

> 2. Gas truck drivers would be required to pass mental and physical examinations by the police traffic division and a physician. Those qualifying would receive a "certificate of fitness." The tests would be patterned after those required in New York City. Fees to be paid by applicants were not detailed;

> 3. All trucks carrying inflammable liquid would be required to carry the wording, "Danger, Inflammable Liquid," in ten-inch letters on the rear and sides of the vehicle, and in four-inch letters on the front bumper.[19]

Hoellen and DuBois disagreed sharply on the issue of compartmentalization of tanks. DuBois, the service station owner, declared compartmented tankers an "economic impossibility" and suggested that the matter be recommended to the state.[20]

Hoellen accused DuBois of passing the buck.

"How many people must die before we do something about a serious problem? There are irresponsible people in the petroleum industry— just as in any other industry."[21]

DuBois offered a rebuttal. "There is too much direction of industry by mandate now. I don't think compartmentation (*sic*) is necessary. Night deliveries would be difficult to accomplish. This would mean increasing the cost of the product. The industry has tried to invite all cooperation for safety. The industry isn't on trial."[22]

Hoellen's ordinance was finally passed in emasculated form by the City Council on November 8, 1951, nearly 1½ years after it was first introduced. In a final humiliation, even the size of the lettering on the gas trucks was reduced from ten inches to just five.[23]

The fitness requirement became the responsibility of Police Commissioner Timothy O'Connor, a burden he did not want for his department. O'Connor argued that the Police Department was not equipped to conduct the examinations. O'Connor suggested to the subcommittee that the Fire Department was better suited to give the examinations. Alderman Pacini referred the matter to Alderman DuBois. According to O'Connor, DuBois agreed to propose the amendment to the Council. But more than six months after the passage of the ordinance, it was reported that little, if anything, had been done in the matter, and the rule regarding certificates of fitness was not being enforced.[24]

The death knell for trolley travel in Chicago sounded long before the early evening of May 25, 1950. It began when the old Chicago Surface Lines had fallen into receivership more than two decades earlier, and the replacement of trolleys and maintenance of hundreds of miles of trolley track had become a financial impossibility.

In 1947, the year the first Green Hornets began chauffeuring passengers along the busiest routes, the CTA began to step up the replacement of older trolleys in favor of motor and trolley buses along other routes.

The trolley buses were relatively new innovations. They ran on electricity and were equipped with twin trolley poles, which allowed them to draw their power from the overhead wires. They also had rubber wheels, giving them more maneuverability than their predecessors, along with the ability to make quicker stops.

The addition of motor buses, which were not confined by the overhead wires, allowed the CTA to extend the length of some of these routes, which increased ridership.

From 1947 to 1949, the CTA began in earnest a conversion of trolley routes into routes for buses and trolley buses. Over the three years, trolleys disappeared from 15 trolley routes on the South Side and a half dozen others on the North Side.[25]

Contrary to public opinion, the May 25 accident had little or no impact on the decision to replace trolleys. It was a high-profile accident that, on the historical timeline, happened to be sandwiched in the middle of the lengthy conversion process, which escalated the following year.

Eleven more routes were converted in 1951, and the Chicago trolley quickly became an endangered species.

Even the Green Hornets, most of them only four or five years old, were gradually removed in favor of buses. In 1953, the Madison line, which had been the first route to use the new, streamlined PCCs in 1936, converted to buses. Seven other lines were converted in 1953, a year in which the CTA managed to finish in the black. That "profit" amounted to a little over $500,000 and was not enough to pay the city its rental fee for use of its streets.[26]

By 1955, only four trolley lines were still operating. That summer, when construction caused an interruption in service along Cottage Grove, the company took advantage of the opportunity to convert the long line to buses. Over 100 trolleys, most of them Green Hornets, were decommissioned. Many were salvaged to build rapid transit cars.

By ending trolley service along Cottage Grove, the CTA saved itself an estimated $300,000 per annum, most of that coming from the elimination of trolley track renovation. By converting just one trolley line, the company saved a figure that was equal to more than half its total profits from a year earlier.[27]

In December 1955, the CTA ended streetcar service on State Street south of downtown, although it continued trolley service on Clark and Broadway for another two years. On the evening of December 5, 1955, the last Green Hornet to travel the No. 36-Broadway/State line passed the obsolete turnaround at 62nd Place. Less than five years after the accident, the trolleys departed from south State Street.[28]

The southern half of the old Clark-Wentworth line remained the only trolley route left in Chicago for about 18 months. Then, on June 21, 1958, Marvin McFall, 54, a veteran CTA motorman, took car No. 7213—a Green Hornet—for a final trip through the circuit—from 81st and Halsted to Kinzie and Clark, and back again. It was the last trolley run in Chicago history. Chicago had once boasted the largest trolley fleet in the world. Now, less than a decade after the Green Hornet Streetcar Disaster, the era of the Chicago trolley was over.[29]

Epilogue

Today, the block-long stretch of State Street between 62nd and 63rd streets is a desolate urban wasteland—one of many on Chicago's South Side. With the exception of bus shelters, billboards, and railroad tracks piled with unused freight cars, no permanent structures are visible for roughly a block. Cracked sidewalks border the thoroughfare. Grass grows in the vacant lot where the turnaround once lay. It is as if the prairie has staked its claim upon the area once again.[1]

On the west side of the street, nestled behind a V-shaped outcropping of billboards, the stone footprint of the Skonicki house pokes out from the prairie grass growing between the sidewalk and the tracks.

Across the street, not a hundred feet away, the decaying entrances to the turnaround are still visible. Pitted and pockmarked, they lead nowhere now, ending where iron pilings have been hammered into the ground along the perimeter of the lot where the turnaround once ran.

The Green Hornet Streetcar Disaster accelerated the decay of the area. Urban blight did the rest. The five buildings left gutted by the fire were leveled by wrecking balls and bulldozers. No other structures ever took their places.

State Street remains a heavily trafficked thoroughfare on the south side of Chicago. Twenty-four hours a day, the CTA operates bus service. The No. 29 bus route runs from 95th Street to the south and Grand Avenue to the north. Every ten minutes or so, a No. 29 passes the vacant lot where the old turnaround loop once operated at 62nd Place. Sixty years removed from the accident, most passengers are unaware of what transpired there.

In the fall of 1955, more than five years after the accident, the CTA paid a $40,000 settlement to survivor Ora Mae Bryant. Bryant had sustained third-degree burns to her arms, neck, and face. While still recovering in the hospital, she received her diploma from the Madam C. J. Walker School of Beauty and Culture.[2]

Bryant's settlement was the last paid by the CTA to a survivor, family member, property owner, or other person injured in some way during the accident. The transit authority wound up paying just under $900,000 in damages to over 150 claimants.

A total of $291,618 in death benefits was paid to family members of the 33 people who died—an average of about $9,250 per claim.

Thirty-seven personal injury cases were settled for a total of $477,076—an average of about $12,000 per claimant. Settlement amounts varied widely. Ora Mae Bryant's settlement was one of the higher awards and reflected the severity of her injuries.

Survivors who signed quickly with ambulance chasers—like the family of Kyteria Cooper—ended up with much smaller settlements.

More than 100 persons were displaced by the fire, which destroyed or severely damaged the buildings in which they lived. Seventy-eight persons received settlements that averaged between $1,000 and $1,500 and totaled $109,062. Just under $5,000 was paid to ten building occupants who suffered injuries during the fire. No claim ever went to trial.[3]

Similar settlements were awarded to survivors and families of victims of the Our Lady of the Angels School fire of December 1958. Although it took seven years to do so, the Archdiocese of Chicago paid death benefits of $7,500 for each of the 92 children who perished in the blaze. The figure for personal injury settlements was substantially higher. Seventy-six claims were settled for about 2.3 million dollars, with an average of just under $30,000 per claimant. As in the Green Hornet case, claims that were filed soon after the event tended to receive smaller awards. The first five claims to be settled received $3,500, $3,500, $14,000, $28,000, and $31,000, respectively.[4]

Once all claims were settled, survivors and family members continued the physical and emotional process of healing. Most remained tight-lipped about the accident, discussing it only with close friends and family members, if at all.

In the spring of 1951, Kyteria Cooper gave birth to a son, born on the one-year anniversary of the accident. Cooper suffered lingering shoulder and back problems throughout her life as a result of her injuries. For a time, she became addicted to prescription pain medications.

Now in her 70s, she uses weekly exercise classes at a local swimming pool to help manage her pain.[5]

After missing work for more than two months, Robert Nalls returned to his job at a North Side bakery. He rode the 36-Broadway/State trolley for the first time since the accident. On his return trip that evening, seconds after passing the turnaround at 62nd Place, the trolley on which he was riding struck an automobile near the entrance to the viaduct. The trolley partially climbed onto the other vehicle. No serious injuries were reported.

Shaken but otherwise unhurt, Nalls had an epiphany.

"This was my first streetcar ride after hospitalization. For this to happen on my first ride—I took (it) as a sign. I never rode the Green Hornet again. I joined church, stopped drinking and hanging out. I will never ever forget this."[6]

Chief Fire Marshal Anthony Mullaney became Chicago's top firefighter in March 1955, being appointed fire commissioner by Mayor Kennelly. He served at the post for two years, retiring in 1957. He died in 1960 at the age of 68.[7]

Chief Michael Ahern remained head of the traffic division until 1956. He was influential in establishing one-way streets throughout the city. After his proposed ban on auto horns in the city failed, he was transferred to the Prairie Avenue Station where he served as commander until his retirement in 1958. He died in 1960 at age 65.[8]

John J. Hoellen served as an alderman until 1975. He twice opposed Richard J. Daley for political office—in 1954 for Cook County commissioner, and in 1975 for mayor. He lost both times.

His good friend and colleague, Democratic alderman Leon Despres, said that Hoellen never lost sight of his reasons for entering politics: "... to fight against corruption and to fight for honest government."

After retiring from politics, Hoellen helped establish the Bank of Ravenswood. He also served for 15 years on the CTA board, retiring in 1990. He died in 1999 at the age of 84.[9]

The Green Hornet Streetcar Disaster launched Steve Lasker on his career as a photojournalist. He was offered more jobs as a result, and he soon began full-time work for *The Chicago Herald-American.*

On the frigid afternoon of December 1, 1958, Lasker stood on the back step of a fire truck and snapped one of the most iconic photographs in Chicago history. The image showed firefighter Richard Scheidt emerging from the smoldering ruins of the Our Lady of the Angels school. In his arms, Scheidt carried the lifeless body of a ten-year-old student.

The photo made front pages across the country. Lasker was nominated for the Pulitzer Prize. He worked for the *Herald-American* until its demise in 1971, and then began a second career as a news cameraman for WBBM-TV in Chicago. He retired in 1996.[10]

Ralph Budd retired as chairman of the CTA in 1952. In his four years with the company, his accomplishments were similar to those he had enjoyed in his decades of service as a railroad executive. He eliminated waste, made day-to-day administration more efficient, and accelerated the modernization of the company's fleet of vehicles.

True to form, he remained active even in retirement. From 1952 to 1953, he chaired a commission that investigated railroads in Brazil. He also continued to serve on several boards of directors, and his duties took him all over the country.

He died in 1962 at the age of 82.[11]

William Liddell's court case went before a judge later that summer. Charged with leaving the scene of an accident, Liddell appeared in Safety Court on July 12.

CTA attorneys representing Liddell managed to get the charge dismissed. Liddell, they argued, was not the motorman of the vehicle. They also reminded the judge that under Illinois law, trolleys were not subject to the same traffic rules as other motor vehicles.[12]

Upon ruling on the motion, Judge Emmett Morrissey expressed some surprise. "Until now, I thought the charge included even wheelbarrows, but I see I was mistaken."[13]

Liddell continued as a conductor with the CTA for several years. In the mid-1950s, he was among the first wave of African-American motormen trained by the CTA. He drove a bus for 25 years, retiring in the late 1970s. He died in 1999.[14]

Charles Kleim also continued his job with the CTA. Diagnosed with diabetes in the late 1950s, he was forced to leave his job as a motorman. He spent the remainder of his CTA career working in a car barn.

He retired to St. Petersburg, Florida, where he passed away in 1986 at the age of 81.[15]

The body of Paul Manning was sent back home to Corinth, Mississippi. After burying her husband, Mamie Manning continued to live with Nell and Ray Medley. Having lost the love of her life, she never remarried, but she reveled in her role as a sort of "second mother" to the Medley children. The trio eventually returned to Corinth. Ray Medley died in 1978.[16]

Mamie remained active into old age, often helping to care for elderly friends and neighbors—many of whom were years younger than she. After Mamie was slowed by a stroke, the two sisters shared a room at a nursing home for a time.[17]

Mamie Manning passed away on April 28, 2008, at the age of 99. Nell Medley followed her sister nearly a year later, in March 2009.[18]

After motor and trolley buses replaced them, the vast majority of Green Hornets employed by the CTA were scavenged for parts that were used to outfit "L" cars. Of the more than 600 Green Hornets employed by the CTA, only one exists today. A fully restored PCC No. 4391 makes daily runs at the Illinois Railway Museum in Union, Illinois. What remained of the Green Hornets was scrapped.[19]

Appendix

VICTIMS OF CTA GREEN HORNET STREETCAR DISASTER

May 25th, 1950, Chicago, Illinois, Cook County

1—Theresa Axtell, 56

2—Marietta Catlin, 21

3— Minnie Banks Dade, 52

4—Clara Dobson, 38

5— Bertha Dowdell, 42

6— George Dowdell, 65

7— Mary Estus, 61

8 — Alean Fisher, 48

9 — Floreine Foster, 21

10—Marie A. Franklin, 41

11—Louis Howlett, 26

12 Martha Mary Jankauskis, 23

13—Tishie Mae Johnson, 23

14— Paul Manning, 42

15—Frances Mennite, 32

16—Daisy Palmer, 23

17—John Penn, 38

18—Luella Phillips, 26

19—Julia Piercefield, 59

20—Annie Richardson, 20

21—Mamie Robinson, 40

22—Caroline Rudenga, 19

23—Rosa Saunders, 37

24—Anna Gordon Schurr, 32

25—Earl Sue Sharp, 56

26—Ollie Smith, 58

27—John E. Storey, 52

28—Dorothy Townsend, 30

29—Douglas Turner, 39

30—Arvis Vos, 20

31—Edward Everett Werner, 65

32—Katie Westerveld, 61

33—Mel Wilson, 39

Notes

ABBREVIATIONS

The accident was well covered by local media. Articles from Chicago's four major daily newspapers and two "twice-weekly's" are liberally cited throughout the text. For convenience, I have abbreviated each as follows:

The Chicago Daily Tribune	CDT
The Chicago Sun-Times	CST
The Chicago Daily News	CDN
The Chicago Herald American	CHA
The Chicago Defender	CDF
The Southtown Economist	TSE

The names of all other sources are cited in their entirety.

CHAPTER ONE

1. Young, David M., *Chicago Transit: An Illustrated History* (DeKalb: Northern Illinois University Press, 1998).

2. CDT, November 2, 1924, 1.

3. Lind, Alan R., *Chicago Surface Lines: An Illustrated History*, 3rd edition (Park Forest: Transport History Press, 1986), 416.

4. CDT, August 24, 1946, 13.

5. CDT, June 9, 1950, 12.

6. CDT, July 6, 1938, 3.

7. CDT, August 12, 1943, 18.

8. CDT, August 23, 1946, 13.

9. Young, *Chicago Transit*, 106.

10. Ibid.

11. CDT, July 7, 1940, S1.

12. Young, *Chicago Transit*, 107.

13. Ibid.

14. CDT, November 20, 1946, 20.

15. Lind, *Chicago Surface Lines*, 101.

16. Williams, Michael, et al., *Chicago: City on the Move* (Chicago: Cityfiles Press, 2007).

17. *Trolley Sparks*, "New Noiseless Cars in Chicago," October 1946, Vol. 2, No. 11.

18. "The PCC Car—Not So Standard," <http://world.nycsubway.org/us/pcc/index.html>

19. Lind, *Chicago Surface Lines*, 104.

20. Ibid.

21. Ibid.

22. Young, *Chicago Transit*, 107.

23. CDN, May 26, 1950, 2.

24. "Car Plans of the Chicago Surface Lines," Electric Railway Historical Society, Bulletin No. 38. Of the 600 cars ordered, 290 were manufactured by the St. Louis Car Co., and 310 were completed by the Pullman Car Co. The St. Louis cars had a seating capacity of 54, while the Pullman cars seated 57. Series numbers 4062–4371 were assigned to the Pullman cars. St. Louis cars were assigned numbers 4052–4061, 4372–4411, and 7035–7274. Paul Manning's car, No. 7078, was built by the St. Louis Car Co., and therefore, had a seating capacity of 54 passengers.

25. CST, May 27, 1950, 3.

26. Ibid.

27. Ibid.

28. Lind, *Chicago Surface Lines*, 105.

29. CDT, June 30, 1950, 10.

30. CDN, May 26, 1950, 31.

31. Ibid.

32. Ibid.

33. CDT, October 28, 1948, B1.

CHAPTER TWO

1. Kelly, R. F., report to James O. Dwight, General Attorney, Chicago Transit Authority, June 30, 1950, henceforth referred to as the "Kelly Report."

2. Ibid.

3. Ibid.

4. Bruce Moffat, interview with author.

5. CHA, June 1, 1950, 2.

6. Bruce Moffat, interview with author.

7. CHA, June 1, 1950, 2.

8. Douglas Kleim, interview with author.

9. CHA, June 1, 1950, 1.

10. Douglas Kleim, interview with author.

11. Kelly Report, Chicago Transit Authority, June 30, 1950.

12. Ibid.

13. Ibid.

14. Ibid.

15. Nell Medley, interview with author.

16. Kelly Report, Chicago Transit Authority, June 30, 1950.

17. CDN, May 27, 1950, 1.

18. CHA, June 1, 1950, 1.

19. CDN, May 27, 1950, 1.

20. Ibid.

21. Elsie Liddell, interview with author.

22. CST, May 26, 1950, 17.

23. CST, May 26, 1950, 10.

CHAPTER THREE

1. TSE, May 28, 1950, 1.

2. CST, May 26, 1950, 6.

3. CDN, May 26, 1950, 1.

4. CDF, May 27, 1950, 1.

5. TSE, May 28, 1950, 1.

6. Ibid.

7. Ibid.

8. Ibid.

9. CST, May 26, 1950, 10.

10. Kyteria Drish, interview with author.

11. Chicago History Museum: Donald O'Toole memoirs and commentaries (manuscript), ca. 1980s. O'Toole was initially hobbled by his own prejudices. He wondered if African-American tenants living in a planned community would live in a responsible manner. He consulted with an associate, Robert Taylor, the future chief of the Chicago Housing Authority, who at the time managed a building on Michigan Avenue that rented to blacks. Taylor assured O'Toole that black tenants would "occupy such a community exactly as would white tenants of equal economic status." The Princeton Park project went ahead as planned.

12. CDT, May 26, 1950, 1.

13. TSE, May 28, 1950, 1.

14. CDF, June 3, 1950, 2.

15. TSE, May 28, 1950, 1.

16. Ibid.

17. Julia Eggebeen, interview with author.

18. Ibid.

19. TSE, May 28, 1950, 1.

20. CDN, May 26, 1950, 5.

21. Kelly Report, Chicago Transit Authority, June 30, 1950.

22. CDT, May 26, 1950, 1.

23. CDN, May 26, 1950, 2.

24. Kelly Report, Chicago Transit Authority, June 30, 1950.

25. Ibid.

26. CHA, June 2, 1950, 2.

27. CST, May 27, 1950, 4.

28. Johanna Skonicki, interview with author.

29. I've extrapolated Skonicki's movements based primarily on his Inquest testimony, as well as comments made in several Chicago papers, including CDN, May 26, 1950, 2.

30. CHA, June 2, 1950, 2.
31. CST, May 27, 1950, 4.
32. CDT, June 2, 1950, 1.
33. CDT, May 26, 1950, 1.
34. CDN, May 26, 1950, 2.
35. Ibid.
36. CDT, May 26, 1950, 1.
37. CDN, May 26, 1950, 2.
38. CDT, May 26, 1950, 1.
39. TSE, May 28, 1950, 1.
40. Ibid.
41. Kyteria Drish, interview with author.
42. Ibid.
43. TSE, May 28, 1950, 1.
44. Ibid.
45. CDT, May 26, 1950, 1.
46. CDT, May 27, 1950, 1.
47. CST, May 27, 1950, 3.
48. CDF, June 3, 1950, 2.
49. CDF, May 27, 1950, 1.

CHAPTER FOUR

1. CST, May 26, 1950, 2.
2. Ibid.
3. CDN, May 26, 1950, 2.
4. TSE, May 28, 1950, 1.
5. CDT, May 26, 1950, 1.
6. CDN, May 26, 1950, 2.
7. Steve Lasker, interview with author.
8. Ibid.
9. Ibid.
10. Ibid.
11. CST, May 26, 1950, 10.
12. Kelly Report, Chicago Transit Authority, June 30, 1950.
13. TSE, May 28, 1950, 1.
14. Ibid.
15. CST, May 26, 1950, 2.
16. TSE, May 28, 1950, 1.
17. Steve Lasker, interview with author.
18. CST, May 26, 1950, 8.
19. Ibid.
20. CDT, May 26, 1950, 1.
21. Kelly Report, Chicago Transit Authority, June 30, 1950.

22. CST, May 26, 1950, 1.

23. Kyteria Drish, interview with authority.

24. TSE, May 28, 1950, 2.

25. Ibid.

26. CST, May 26, 1950, 6.

27. TSE, May 28, 1950, 2.

28. CDF, May 27, 1950, 1.

29. CST, May 26, 1950, S8.

30. Ibid.

31. Ibid.

32. CDF, June 3, 1950, 19.

33. Ibid.

34. Ibid.

35. Ibid.

CHAPTER FIVE

1. CDN, May 26, 1950, 1.

2. Ibid.

3. CDT, May 26, 1950, 1.

4. Ibid.

5. Johanna Skonicki, interview with author.

6. CDN, May 26, 1950, 3.

7. CST, May 26, 1950, 2.

8. TSE, May 28, 1950, 1.

9. Ibid.

10. CST, May 25, 1950, 6.

11. Ibid.

12. CDN, May 31, 1950, 1.

13. Ibid.

14. Ibid.

15. Ibid.

16. Ibid.

17. Ibid.

18. Ibid.

19. CDN, May 31, 1950, 1. Krasnow was one of more than a dozen attorneys and runners whose names appeared in local papers in an effort to discourage ambulance chasers.

20. Kyteria Drish, interview with author.

21. CDN, June 2, 1950, 2.

22. CDT, May 26, 1950, 3.

23. Ibid.

24. Julia Eggebeen, interview with author.

25. CDN, May 26, 1950, 8.

26. Ibid.

27. Ibid.

28. Ibid.

29. CDT, May 26, 1950, 8.

30. Ibid.

31. CST, May 27, 1950, 3.

32. CDN, May 26, 1950, 8.

33. Nell Medley, interview with author.

34. CDT, May 29, 1950, 6.

CHAPTER SIX

1. Young, *Chicago Transit*, 122.

2. Overton, Richard C., "The Railway and Locomotive Historical Society Bulletin, No. 106," University of Western Ontario, April 1962, 82–85.

3. Ibid.

4. Ibid.

5. Ibid.

6. CDT, September 2, 1949, 4.

7. CDT, June 28, 1950, 9.

8. Ibid.

9. CST, May 26, 1950, 6.

10. CST, May 26, 1950, 10.

11. CST, May 27, 1950, 2.

12. Ibid.

13. Ibid.

14. Ibid.

15. Ibid.

16. CDT, May 26, 1950, 1.

17. Ibid.

18. CST, May 26, 1950, 2.

19. CDT, May 26, 1950, 1.

20. CST, May 27, 1950, 3.

21. Ibid.

22. Ibid.

23. Ibid.

24. Ibid.

25. Ibid.

26. CDT, May 27, 1950, 1.

27. Ibid.

28. Adding to the confusion of Liddell's post-accident whereabouts were two articles published on the same day. *The Chicago Sun-Times* (May 26, 1950, 2) reported that Liddell "disappeared mysteriously" after giving his statement to CTA officials. Liddell presumably had time to talk to reporters before leaving. *The*

Sun-Times also printed Liddell's own account of his efforts in opening the rear doors. A similar story appeared off the UP wire service (*United Press*, May 26, 1950) in which CTA officials permitted Liddell to make a brief statement to the media, "then spirited him away."

29. CST, May 27, 1950, 2.
30. CDN, May 27, 1950, 1.
31. Ibid.
32. Ibid.
33. Ibid.
34. Ibid.
35. CST, May 28, 1950, 3.
36. Ibid.
37. Ibid.
38. CDF, June 3, 1950, 3.
39. CDF, June 10, 1950, 3.
40. CDF, June 3, 1950, 8.
41. CDF, June 3, 1950, 1.
42. Elsie Liddell, interview with author.
43. CDN, June 3, 1950, 1.
44. CDN, May 29, 1950, 1.
45. CDF, June 3, 1950, 2.

CHAPTER SEVEN

1. CDT, August 28, 1952, 14.
2. Ibid.
3. CDT, June 15, 1946, 5.
4. CDT, June 1, 1950, 1.
5. CDT, June 2, 1950, 1.
6. CHA, June 1, 1950, 1.
7. Ibid.
8. Ibid.
9. CDT, June 2, 1950, 1.
10. CHA, June 1, 1950, 1.
11. Ibid.
12. Ibid.
13. Ibid.
14. Ibid.
15. CDT, May 27, 1950, 1.
16. CHA, June 2, 1950, 2.
17. Ibid.
18. Ibid.
19. CDF, June 3, 1950, 4.
20. Ibid.

21. CHA, June 2, 1950, 2.
22. CDN, June 2, 1950, 2.
23. CDN, June 2, 1950, 3.
24. CHA, June 3, 1950, 3.
25. Ibid.
26. Ibid.
27. Ibid.
28. CST, June 2, 1950, 3.
29. Ibid.
30. CHA, June 1, 1950, 2.
31. CDF, June 3, 1950, 1.
32. CDN, May 26, 1950, 8.
33. CST, June 2, 1950, 3.
34. CDN, June 1, 1950, 3.
35. CST, June 2, 1950, 3.
36. CHA, June 1, 1950, 2.
37. CST, June 2, 1950, 3.
38. CDN, June 1, 1950, 3.
39. CDT, June 2, 1950, 2.
40. CDF, June 3, 1950, 4.
41. CDT, June 2, 1950, 2.
42. CST, June 2, 1950, 3.
43. CDN, June 2, 1950, 3.
44. CHA, June 2, 1950, 1.
45. CDT, June 2, 1950, 1.
46. Ibid.
47. Telescoping claimed many lives during the Illinois Central Gulf commuter rail crash, which occurred on the cloudy morning of October 30, 1972, in Chicago. A new, bi-level commuter train loaded with passengers and heading into downtown Chicago overshot a station and began backing up. In passing beyond the platform, the train had already tripped sensors, which gave the "all clear" signal to the next train on the line, an older, heavier express. The express struck the bi-level train at full speed, telescoping about half way through the rear car. Forty-five passengers, most of them on board the bi-level train, were killed and 332 were injured. It was Chicago's worst rail disaster. (National Transportation Safety Board. *Railroad Accident Report: Collision of Illinois Central Gulf Railroad Commuter Trains, Chicago, Illinois, October 30, 1971.* Report #NTSB RAR-73-5.)
48. CDT, June 2, 1950, 1.
49. Ibid.
50. CST, June 2, 1950, 3.
51. CDN, June 2, 1950, 31.
52. CST, June 2, 1950, 3.
53. CDT, June 2, 1950, 1.
54. CDT, June 2, 1950, 1.

55. Ibid.
56. Ibid.
57. Ibid.

CHAPTER EIGHT

1. CST, May 28, 1950, 22.
2. Ibid.
3. CDT, February 1, 1999, 6.
4. Ibid.
5. CDT, June 9, 1950, 12.
6. Ibid.
7. Ibid.
8. Ibid.
9. CDT, June 23, 1950, 17.
10. CDT, June 16, 1950, 1.
11. CDT, June 23, 1950, 17.
12. Ibid.
13. Ibid.
14. Ibid.
15. Ibid.
16. CDT, June 21, 1950, 1.
17. Ibid.
18. Ibid.
19. Ibid.
20. Ibid. Budd made the latter comment in response to calls for push-out windows on the trolley. He felt that passengers might feel the temptation to use such windows in non-emergency situations.
21. Kelly Report, Chicago Transit Authority, June 30, 1950.
22. Ibid.
23. Ibid.
24. Ibid.
25. Ibid.
26. Ibid.
27. Ibid.
28. Ibid.
29. Elsie Liddell, interview with author.
30. Kelly Report, Chicago Transit Authority, June 30, 1950.
31. Ibid.
32. Ibid.
33. Ibid.
34. Ibid.
35. Ibid.
36. Ibid.

37. Ibid.
38. Ibid.
39. Ibid.
40. Ibid.

CHAPTER NINE

1. "Conclusions and Recommendations of the Coroner's Jury Investigating the South State Street Accident of May 25, 1950," released June 29, 1950.
2. Ibid.
3. Ibid.
4. Ibid.
5. Ibid.
6. Ibid.
7. Ibid.
8. Ibid.
9. Ibid.
10. Ibid.
11. Ibid.
12. CST, May 27, 1950, 2.
13. CDT, February 9, 1952, 10.
14. CDT, August 26, 1952, 20.
15. CDT, December 29, 1953, 8.
16. CDT, November 16, 1954, 1.
17. CDT, February 9, 1952, 10.
18. Ibid.
19. CDT, September 14, 1951, A7.
20. Ibid.
21. Ibid.
22. Ibid.
23. CDT, June 30, 1952, 12.
24. Ibid.
25. Lind, *Chicago Surface Lines.*
26. CDT, June 7, 1955, 10.
27. Ibid.
28. Lind, *Chicago Surface Lines*, 306.
29. Williams, et al., *Chicago, City on the Move*, 180.

EPILOGUE

1. My observation.
2. CDT, September 30, 1955, 5.
3. CDT, October 3, 1955, 22.
4. Cowan, David, and John Kuenster, *To Sleep with the Angels* (Chicago:

Ivan R. Dee, 1996), 240.

5. Kyteria Drish, interview with author.

6. Robert Nalls, letter to author.

7. CDT, November 29, 1960, B11.

8. CDT, March 12, 1960, 16.

9. CDT, February 1, 1999, 6.

10. Steve Lasker, interview with author.

11. Overton, Richard C., University of Western Ontario, "The Railway and Locomotive Historical Society Bulletin, No. 106," April 1962, 82–85.

12. CDT, July 13, 1950, B8.

13. Ibid.

14. Elsie Liddell, interview with author.

15. Douglas Kleim, interview with author.

16. Nell Medley, interview with author.

17. Ibid.

18. Mike Medley, interview with author.

19. Lind, *Chicago Surface Lines*, 109.

Selected Bibliography

Cowan, David. *Great Chicago Fires.* Chicago: Lake Claremont Press, 2001.

Cowan, David, and John Kuenster. *To Sleep with the Angels: The Story of a Fire.* Chicago: Ivan R. Dee, 1996.

Grossman, James R., Ann Durkin Keating, and Janice L. Reiff. *The Encyclopedia of Chicago.* Chicago: University of Chicago Press, 2004.

Lind, Alan R. *Chicago Surface Lines: An Illustrated History.* Park Forest: Transport History Press, 3rd edition, 1986.

Roberts, Maria L., and Robert Stamz. *Chicago's Englewood Neighborhood: At the Junction.* Chicago: Arcadia Publishing, 2002.

Williams, Michael, Richard Cahan, and Bruce Moffat. *Chicago: City on the Move.* Chicago: Cityfiles Press, 2007.

Young, David M. *Chicago Transit: An Illustrated History.* DeKalb: Northern Illinois University Press, 1998.

Index